W9-CPH-423

Combination Crafts ™

Edited by Vicki Blizzard

HOUSE of
WHITE
BIRCHES
PUBLISHERS
SINCE 1947

Combination Crafts™

Copyright © 2004 House of White Birches,
Berne, Indiana 46711
The publisher grants permission to create and sell the craft projects featured in this book.

Editor: Vicki Blizzard
Associate Editor: Lisa M. Fosnaugh
Contributing Editor: Maria Nerius
Technical Editor: Läna Schurb
Copy Editors: Michelle Beck, Nicki Lehman
Publication Coordinator: June Sprunger

Photography: Tammy Christian, Kelly Heydinger, Christena Green
Photo Stylist: Tammy Nussbaum

Art Director: Brad Snow
Publishing Services Manager: Brenda Gallmeyer
Graphic Arts Supervisor: Ronda Bechinski
Book Design: Amy S. Lin
Graphic Artist/Cover Design: Edith Teegarden
Production Assistants: Marj Morgan
Technical Artists: Chad Summers

Chief Executive Officer: John Robinson
Publishing Director: David McKee
Book Marketing Director: Craig Scott
Editorial Director: Vivian Rothe

Printed in the United States of America
First Printing: 2004
Library of Congress Number: 2003108834
ISBN: 1-59217-036-6

Every effort has been made to ensure the accuracy and completeness of the instructions in this book. However, we cannot be responsible for human error or for the results when using materials other than those specified in the instructions, or for variations in individual work.

Dear Crafter,

All of us have a closet full of unused craft supplies. You know the ones: extra wooden shapes from a child's project, leftover acrylic paint from the decorative tray you painted as a gift, the remaining feathers in a package when you only needed three for your last project, or the fabric remnants on sale at a price too good to resist. And what do you do with all the glitter left in the big bottle you had to purchase to get the color you needed for the Christmas cards you just created? Face it, we all have bits and pieces of this and that. The hard part is figuring out how to combine these scrap materials to create stunning projects.

That's where this book comes in. For each section, we gave our designers a very specific list of materials they could work with. They were free to choose their working surface, and they were allowed to add two additional craft products that weren't on our list. We are so pleased with what they created; their unique designs are very trendy and very wonderful, and really showcase all the different things that can be created with the same materials!

As further inspiration, we created a special assignment for three designers with very different styles, which we call our Designer Challenge. For each section in this book, we mailed each of them the same package of craft materials, including their working surface. They were allowed to choose two additional products to use for their designs. They've created some outstanding projects that we hope will inspire you to create using your own materials.

Your creativity is really what this book is all about. Our ultimate goal is to inspire you to look through your own stash of supplies and see what you can use to create the projects in this book. Don't have the fibers our designers used in the second section? Substitute ribbon instead. Don't have square wooden shapes? How about using round ones instead? Ultrafine glitter can be used in place of chunky glitter—or vice versa! Let your imagination run wild, and let your inspiration be what you have on hand in your craft closets!

Happy crafting,

Vicki Blizzard

Contents

6 Woodsies, Glitter, Stickers & Spray Paint

Put together this unlikely combination of products to create projects that will surprise and delight you with their finished look!

26 Beads, Wire, Fibers, Paper Clay, Powdered Pigments

Everyone has a little of each of these materials in their craft closets. Pull out these products now and combine them in unique ways!

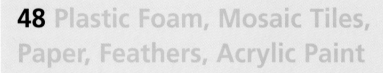

48 Plastic Foam, Mosaic Tiles, Paper, Feathers, Acrylic Paint

How in the world can you combine feathers with mosaic tiles? Flip through the pages of this section to find out!

70 Rubber Stamps, Polymer Clay, Embossing Powders, Metal Sheets, Glass Paint

Use your rubber stamps for unique projects that aren't cards or scrapbook pages! You'll be amazed at what you can create with this assortment of products.

92 Stencils, Stamping Ink Pads, Jewels & Gems

You'll find everything from a unique torchère lamp to a glitzy evening bag in this section. Don't want to make an evening bag? Use the same technique to create a jacket or a wall hanging!

112 Fabric, Window-Cling Paints

Our designers have come up with outstanding projects for an unlikely combination of craft products. You'll be surprised at how many different ways window cling paint can be used!

138 Paper, Markers, Metallic Paints, Felt

We all have oodles of leftover markers and paint. Combine them with paper and felt to create treasured projects!

160 Rub-On Transfers, Florals, Leather & Suede, Acrylic Paints

Create one-of-a-kind projects with an unexpected combination of craft materials. Add your personal touch by substituting materials you already have on hand!

WOODSIES
Glitter
Stickers
SPRAY PAINT

Excitement abounds when you
learn how to combine these
materials in unique ways. You'll
want to create each of these
special projects!

Words to Inspire Clock

The challenge—each designer needs to create a project using the materials we selected (and one or two more items they add).

Design by June Fiechter

When I saw the interesting shape of this clock, I wondered, How can I make it look like a grandfather clock with the bottom closed in? What a simple solution to use fabric! As I looked through the sticker selection, I was inspired to go with a dreamy theme featuring stars and uplifting words. The colors seem relaxing to me.

—**June Fiechter**

Materials
- Walnut Hollow Open Base Pendulum Clock
- Walnut Hollow Pendulum Clock Movement Kit
- Design Master spray primer
- Design Master spray paints: pink, blue, green, yellow
- Woodsies wooden cutout stars from Forster: 3 (1¾-inch), 4 (1¼-inch), 9 (¾-inch)
- Fabric
- Magic Scraps glitter: fine yellow *and* green; blue Shaved Ice
- Fabri-Tac glue from Beacon Adhesives
- Stickers
- Foam brush
- Mod Podge decoupage glue/ sealer from Plaid

Instructions

1 Cut fabric to fit neatly around pillars of clock, adding an extra ½ inch of fabric for folding under when gluing. Glue fabric to pillars only along top and bottom, folding edge of fabric under while pulling it smooth and taut.

2 Referring to "Spray Painting Made Simple" (General Instructions, page 174) throughout, spray entire clock with primer; let dry.

3 Spray clock with green, blue, pink and yellow paints, applying several coats to fabric. Let dry.

4 Paint wooden stars with decoupage glue/sealer and, while still wet, sprinkle with yellow glitter; set aside to dry. (See "Spray Painting Made Simple," General Instructions, page 174.)

5 Apply desired stickers over surface of fabric and clock.

6 Coat clock, including stickers, with decoupage glue/sealer. While still wet, sprinkle piece with blue flakes and green glitter; let dry.

7 Coat entire clock with decoupage glue/sealer; let dry.

8 Using fabric glue, attach four small stars at 12, 3, 6 and 9 o'clock positions as shown. Glue remaining stars randomly to clock.

9 Brush clock hands with fabric glue; while still wet, sprinkle with yellow glitter. Let dry, making sure glue does not drip and "freeze" hands in position; tap off excess glitter.

10 Assemble clock according to manufacturer's instructions. ◆

Craft Closet Challenge

Time for Jewelry

Design by Judi Kauffman

Instructions

1 Referring to photo throughout, layer and glue wooden cutouts:

Eyes (make a left and a right, keeping pointed end of large leaf shape at outer edge): eyelashes: large triangle; eyebrow: large oval; eyeball: large leaf, large, medium and small circles. Glue to clock face.

Hair: Glue assorted stars to points of nine large leaves; glue leaves' round ends to back of clock face.

Ears (make a left and a right): Layer large circle on large square; glue onto large oval.

Materials

- Walnut Hollow Open Base Pendulum Clock
- Walnut Hollow Pendulum Clock Movement Kit
- Assorted Woodsies cutouts from Forster: triangles, hearts, leaves, ovals, squares, circles
- Quick-setting glue
- Design Master spray paints: ice blue, lavender, purple
- Magic Scraps glitter: fine hot pink; blue Shaved Ice
- Paintbrushes: 2 (1-inch), 2 (1½-inch)
- Paint pens: black, gold, white
- Alphabet stickers
- Spray primer
- Foam brush
- Mod Podge decoupage glue/sealer from Plaid
- Fabric glue

Earrings: Layer large and medium hearts, aligning points; top with small circle. Glue earrings onto ear lobes (lower end of large oval on ears). Glue ears and earrings to back of clock face, just below hair.

Hearts at shoulders: Glue three medium triangles in a stack. Glue stack between two large hearts, keeping sides flush. Glue to front of face near bottom as shown.

Leaf necklace: Glue five leaves across top front edge of clock base. Add four more leaves, raised on medium circles for dimension.

Triangular trim at bottom: Glue five medium triangles across bottom edge of clock base.

Arms and feet: Glue 2-inch paintbrushes to back of clock face so that they stick out like arms (make sure ends of brushes do not extend into slot for pendulum). Glue 1-inch brushes to wooden ball feet at bottom of clock.

2 Cover metal and brush portions of paintbrushes with plastic wrap.

Referring to "Spray Painting Made Simple" (General Instructions, page 174), spray entire clock with several light coats of lavender. Randomly spray arms, base and dowels with ice blue; spray hair with two coats ice blue. Darken cheeks and leaves and randomly spray base and feet with purple.

3 Referring to "Save That Glitter!" (General Instructions, page 174), glue hot pink fine glitter around "wrists" just below metal ferule on arm paintbrushes to form bracelets. Glue blue flake glitter to stars in hair.

4 Remove plastic wrap from brushes. Using paint pens, add details to face, earrings, wrists, leaf garland and triangles at base as shown.

5 Assemble clock according to manufacturer's instructions. Add stickers to pendulum as desired. ◆

Immediately after the box of supplies arrived, I put the clock flat on my table and started playing with the Woodsies shapes. As I started layering them, the idea of a face emerged, and my imagination was off and running. The dimensional hearts by the face and the leaf necklace didn't occur to me till late in the process. At first I was going to make hands out of a pair of child's leather gloves, but without arms they looked all wrong. A paintbrush nearby led me to the idea of brushes for arms and feet. The arms became the perfect place to hang bracelets and necklaces, and the area in front of the face looked like the logical perch for rings.

—**Judi Kauffman**

Playtime Pendulum Clock

Design by Mary Lynn Maloney

Instructions

1 Referring to "Spray Painting Made Simple" (General Instructions, page 174), spray entire clock with four to six light, even coats of coral. In same fashion, spray five 1¼-inch circles and one ¾-inch circle yellow; spray one 1¼-inch, one 2-inch and two ¾-inch circles ice blue; spray one 1¼-inch circle, one 2-inch circle and two ¾-inch circles pink glow; spray remaining circles holiday green. Let dry.

2 Using stickers, spell out "play" on four 1¼-inch yellow circles, pressing stickers firmly into place. Brush with a light coat of varnish; let dry.

Materials

- Walnut Hollow Open Base Pendulum Clock
- Walnut Hollow Pendulum Clock Movement Kit
- Design Master spray paints: coral, yellow, purple, pink glow, ice blue, holiday green
- Woodsies wooden cutout circles from Forster: 6 (¾-inch), 9 (1¼-inch), 4 (2-inch)
- Pathways Alphabet Overlay Stickers from Provo Craft
- Magic Scraps glitter: fine green; light green Shaved Ice
- Decorative trim: 3 yards pink, 18 inches orange-green multicolored
- 1 yard orange-pink-yellow multicolored beaded fringe
- Clear-drying tacky glue
- Satin varnish
- Paintbrush

3 Referring to "Save That Glitter!" (General Instructions, page 174), apply a bead of tacky glue in incised circle of clock face and sprinkle with fine green glitter. Shake off excess. Apply a bead of glue along front edges of top and bottom platforms on clock base; sprinkle with light green flake-style glitter; shake off excess.

4 Apply a bead of glue just outside green glitter circle on clock face; press multicolored trim into glue. Cut a 21-inch piece of pink trim; glue around outside edge of clock face. Cut two 23-inch pieces of pink trim; glue one around top platform of clock base and the other around bottom platform, above lines of glitter.

5 Cut a 23-inch piece of beaded fringe trim; adhere to underside of top platform of clock base.

6 Glue "play" circles onto different-color 2-inch circles; glue letters at 12, 3, 6 and 9 o'clock positions on clock face. Glue a pink and a blue ¾-inch circle onto green 1¼-inch circle. Glue assembled pieces in center of bottom platform's front edge.

7 Glue remaining painted circles onto clock face, alternating colors and shapes.

8 Assemble clock following manufacturer's instructions. ◆

> *I don't normally use much glitter in my design work, so this project really was a challenge! I decided to just get really playful with the colors and glitz, and the result is this fun, whimsical piece.*
> —**Mary Lynn Maloney**

Fantasy Dragonfly Candleholders

Whimsical dragonflies take on an uptown look when created in a silver and gold color palette.

Designs by Sandy L. Rollinger

Materials

Each Candleholder

- Ceramic square column candle or tea-light holder
- Spray paints: metallic gold, matte metallic silver
- Holographic or glittery gold border-strip stickers
- Gold glitter
- Jewel glue
- 3 wooden craft sticks
- 4 wooden medium teardrop-shape cutouts
- Glass cleaner
- Wire nippers *or* craft cutters

Instructions

1 Clean candleholder with glass cleaner; let dry.

2 Referring to "Spray Painting Made Simple" (General Instructions, page 174), spray candleholder with an even, light coat of silver hammered metal paint; let dry. Repeat as necessary to cover completely.

3 Using wire nippers, cut two craft sticks in half. Referring to photo throughout, glue teardrop on end of each stick to form wings, leaving a small space in the center of each stick to accommodate body. Glue long stick (body) to center; let dry.

4 Spray front of dragonfly with gold paint; let dry. Repeat on backside.

5 Cut a length of gold border sticker to fit across each wing; press into place.

6 Referring to "Save That Glitter!" (General Instructions, page 174), apply dots of glue to wings; shake on gold glitter. Apply glue down length of body; shake on glitter. Let dry; then shake off excess.

7 Glue dragonfly to candleholder. ◆

> *I have dragonflies around my pond, and I love watching them glisten in the sunlight. What better way to make my dragonflies glisten than to apply glitter to them? I felt the candleholders would be a great vehicle for them. I can see them glisten in the soft flame of a candle in the evening on my patio.*
>
> —Sandy L. Rollinger

Dresden Set

Ultrafine glitter creates the look of frosted glass and gently softens the colors of this Victorian-inspired set.

Designs by Samantha McNesby

Materials

Each Project
- Ivory spray paint
- White super-fine diamond glitter
- Satin-finish sealer
- 1-inch sponge brush
- Thick white craft glue *or* hot-glue gun
- Cardboard scrap *or* large box
- Scrap paper

Box
- 7 x 4-inch oval papier-mâché box with lid
- About 24 (⅜-inch) wooden circle cutouts
- Victorian-style floral stickers: 1 large, 2 small
- Pink craft paint
- ½-inch flat brush

Frame
- 8-inch-square wooden frame with square opening
- Wooden cutouts: about 15 (¾-inch) circles, about 17 (1¼-inch) circles
- Medium pink spray paint
- 4 large Victorian-style floral stickers
- Pink craft paint
- ¾-inch-wide low-tack tape
- ½-inch flat brush

Each Ornament
- Wooden cutouts: about 16 medium teardrops or medium circles, 2 (3-inch) circles
- Medium pink or blue spray paint
- 2 pink or blue floral stickers
- 8 inches ⅜-inch-wide sheer white ribbon

Box

1. Referring to "Spray Painting Made Simple" (General Instructions, page 174), spray box and lid with a light, even coat of ivory paint. Let dry. Add another coat or two.

2. Spray-paint wooden cutouts; let dry.

3. Trim white borders from edges of stickers. Affix sticker(s) to box lid as shown, pressing into place.

4. Using ½-inch flat brush, paint edge of box lid pink; paint vertical pink stripes on sides of box; let dry.

5. Glue cutouts around edges of box lid; let dry.

6. Refer to "Save That Glitter!" in the General Instructions, page 174. Using sponge brush, coat box lid with sealer. While sealer is still wet, sprinkle lid with glitter. Let dry, then tap to remove excess.

7. Referring to step 6, coat exterior of box with sealer and add glitter.

Frame

1. Referring to "Spray Painting Made Simple" (General Instructions, page 174), spray frame with a light, even coat of ivory paint; let dry. Repeat once or twice.

2. Follow same procedure to paint wooden cutouts medium pink; let dry.

3. Carefully center a strip of tape down front of frame. Place a strip of tape on each side of the first with edges just touching. Repeat to cover entire frame with tape, then peel off every other strip.

4. Mix three parts pink craft paint with one part water. Load ½-inch flat brush with mixture. Crumple a paper towel; have it ready to blot paint. Paint one exposed stripe of wood with paint mixture and, while paint is still wet, blot lightly with paper towel, allowing some of the color to remain. Working on one stripe at a time, continue in this manner until all exposed stripes have been painted and blotted. Let

Over the years I have collected a lot of Victorian-style floral stickers, so I decided my projects for this chapter would have a Victorian "shabby chic" theme. Victorian made me think of the lovely antique Dresden Christmas ornaments often featured in Victorian-style catalogs and decorating magazines. Dresden ornaments are from Germany and feature ground-glass glitter over Victorian-style paper cuts and paintings. By substituting stickers from my collection for the paper cuts and fine art glitter for the ground glass, my box, ornaments and frame were well on their way!

—Samantha McNesby

dry, then carefully peel away remaining tape.

5 Using same mixture and painting-blotting technique, paint sides of frame; let dry.

6 Trim white borders from edges of stickers. Affix stickers to each side of frame, centering them carefully.

7 Glue round cutouts to back of frame as shown, allowing about half of each circle to extend beyond edge of frame.

8 Referring to "Save That Glitter!" (General Instructions, page 174), use sponge brush to coat frame with sealer. While still wet, sprinkle frame with glitter. Let dry, then tap frame to remove any excess.

Pink Ornament

1 Referring to "Spray-Painting Made Simple" (General Instructions, page 174), spray round wooden cutouts with a light, even coat of ivory paint. Let dry. Repeat once or twice.

2 Follow same procedure to paint wooden teardrops pink. When dry, turn teardrops over and paint other surface.

3 Trim white borders from edges of pink stickers. Affix a sticker to center of each 3-inch circle as shown.

4 Place one circle on flat work surface, right side down. Glue teardrops around circle with rounded portion extending beyond edge.

5 Fold ribbon in half; knot ends together. Glue knot on back of ornament, leaving ribbon loop free for hanging.

6 Lay second circle on top of first, right side up, sandwiching knot

and points of teardrop shapes in between. Glue second circle in place; let dry.

7 Referring to "Save That Glitter!" (General Instructions, page 174), use sponge brush to coat one side of ornament with sealer. While still wet, sprinkle ornament with glitter. Let dry, then tap ornament to remove any excess.

8 Coat other side of ornament with sealer and add glitter.

Blue Ornament
Follow instructions for pink ornament, substituting blue paint and stickers. ◆

Dream Frame

Soft colors of paint and glitter create a dreamy piece in which to display your favorite photo.

Design by Mary Ayres

Materials
- 7 x 9-inch wooden frame
- 5 (1-inch) square wooden cutouts
- ⅝-inch black alphabet stickers
- Iridescent ultrafine glitter
- Satin spray paint: white, slate blue
- 4.5mm clear rhinestones
- 2 (8½ x 11-inch) thin plastic sheets (or plastic folders from an office supply store)
- Clear-drying white craft glue
- Medium round bristle paintbrush
- Small sponge

Instructions

1 Referring to "Spray-Painting Made Simple" (General Instructions, page 174), spray frame and squares white. Let dry.

2 *Cloud stencils:* Using patterns provided, cut rounded pattern near bottom edge of one plastic sheet; cut a concave pattern from remaining sheet.

3 *Paint clouds:* Position rounded cloud stencil close to bottom of frame. Lightly spray slate blue across top of stencil. Remove stencil; let dry. Turn stencil over; move it above and slightly to left or right, so different cloud pattern is above first; lightly spray slate blue across top. Remove stencil; let dry.

I have never used spray paint before, but I could picture creating soft clouds from the fine spray. I wanted to keep all the design elements soft, so I used a very neutral palette of colors. I love working with Woodsies. Crafters tend to use them for kids' crafts, but I think the thin wooden shapes are perfect for more elegant designs.

—Mary Ayres

4 Referring to step 3, cover frame with clouds. Clouds will be darker at top.

5 Place concave cloud stencil above second set of clouds on bottom of frame, aligning edge of stencil with edge of clouds; lightly spray white across bottom of stencil (you do not need to spray first set of clouds because they are already white).

6 Continue moving stencil and spraying white paint across top of each grouping of clouds, keeping edges soft. If paint gets too heavy in spots, place concave and rounded stencils above and below cloud area and lightly spray with white or slate blue, depending on which color is too heavy.

7 Referring to photo throughout, affix alphabet stickers to wooden squares to spell "DREAM," positioning letters on the diagonal.

8 Referring to "Save That Glitter!" (General Instructions, page 174) and working with one square at a time, sponge glue evenly onto front of square, then quickly sprinkle with glitter and shake off excess.

9 Place rounded stencil on edge of bottom cloud shape on frame. Place concave stencil slightly above rounded one, leaving a small space between stencils. Dab dry brush into glue, then dab space between stencils with brush. Quickly sprinkle glitter onto glue and shake off excess. Repeat for each cloud shape. There will be an edge of glitter on the top of each cloud shape.

10 Glue wooden squares across top of frame to spell "DREAM." Weight with heavy book or similar object so shapes don't warp as they dry.

11 Glue rhinestones to tips of squares and randomly around frame. ◆

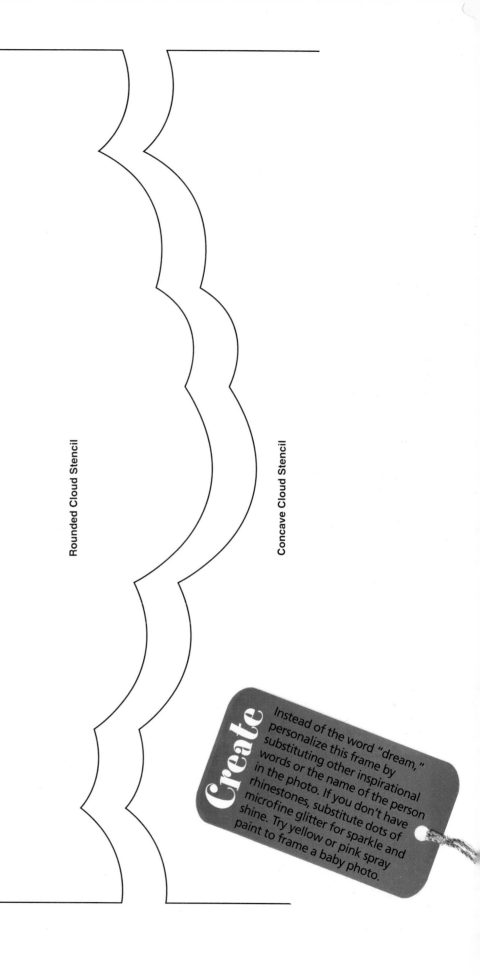

Rounded Cloud Stencil

Concave Cloud Stencil

Create Instead of the word "dream," personalize this frame by substituting other inspirational words or the name of the person in the photo. If you don't have rhinestones, substitute dots of microfine glitter for sparkle and shine. Try yellow or pink spray paint to frame a baby photo.

Collaged Garden Journal

Keep track of your gardening progress in a journal adorned with nature stickers and handmade paper.

Design by Chris Malone

Materials

- 10-inch square journal or scrapbook with cardboard covers and spiral wire binder
- Wooden cutouts: 8 (1-inch) squares, 6 (1½-inch) squares, 2 (2-inch) squares, 2 (2½-inch) circles, 3¼-inch oval, 2⅝-inch oval
- Caramel suede-finish textured spray paint
- Acrylic spray paint: cream, moss green
- Brown alphabet stickers with 1-inch uppercase letters and ½-inch lowercase letters, and sticker with word "our"
- Flower and butterfly stickers
- Garden saying on clear paper
- Gold fine glitter
- Gold microbeads
- Decorative papers: brown, cream, green, pale green
- Assorted fibers in coordinating colors: yarns, pearl cotton, cord, narrow ribbon, braids
- Spray matte finish
- Paintbrush
- Drill with small bit
- Craft glue
- Glue with tip applicator
- Large-eye needle

Instructions

1 Referring to "Spray Painting Made Simple" (General Instructions, page 174), spray journal covers with one coat of textured paint. Add second coat as necessary for good coverage. *Note: If desired, remove covers before painting by turning coils until book is unthreaded. Re-assemble when paint is dry.*

2 Spray 1-inch and 1½-inch squares, one circle and larger oval with one coat cream paint; spray remaining cutouts green. Let dry; add second coat as necessary.

3 Drill hole in one corner of large square and at one end of circle and smaller oval to use these pieces as tags. Drill hole in both ends of larger oval.

4 Spray cutouts with two light coats of matte finish, letting finish dry between coats; keep holes open.

5 Center uppercase letter stickers to spell "GARDEN" on cream 1½-inch squares; press firmly. In same manner, apply stickers to spell "journal" on seven 1-inch cream squares; place "our" sticker on remaining 1-inch cream square.

6 Select flower and butterfly stickers to decorate remaining wooden cutouts. Press each securely in place.

7 Cut 4¼ x 6¾-inch rectangle from green paper. Tear remaining paper as follows: 4½ x 8½-inch piece brown, 2½ x 5½-inch piece cream, 2½-inch square from pale green. Referring to photo throughout, arrange papers on front cover. Apply garden saying to cut green rectangle; glue papers in place.

8 Thread a few fibers through holes in large oval tag (use large-eye needle if necessary); knot ends and clip to 1½ inches. Glue three cutouts with stickers to front cover. Glue "GARDEN" and "journal" squares to brown paper background. Glue "our" square on top of larger "G" and "A" squares.

9 *Make fiber tie:* Cut a variety of fibers 14 inches long. Fold bundle in half and slip loop through wire coil at top of binder. Pull ends through loop and tighten. Attach three stickered tags to different fibers, threading fiber through hole and knotting end. Clip excess close to knot. Vary hanging length of each tag.

10 Referring to "Save That Glitter!" (General Instructions, page 174), use applicator tip to apply glue to selected areas of flower stickers—centers, bases of leaves, etc. Cover with microbeads; let dry, then shake off excess. Apply glue to knot on fiber tie and fibers on oval tag; sprinkle with fine glitter. Let dry, then shake off excess. ◆

"When I start thinking about how to plan a project with a given collection of products, I like to include the surface I might use. I write a list of all kinds of possible end products that are trendy and useful; then I start sketching (more like doodling!). The Woodsies seemed to fit well with the popular paper crafts of scrapbooking and collage-making because they remind me of tags, so the idea of a journal came to mind. A visit to the sticker section of the local scrapbook store sold me on a gardening theme."

—Chris Malone

our GARDEN Journal

There is no unbelief. Whoever plants a seed beneath the sod And waits to see it push away the clod. He trusts in God.

KATE DOUGLAS WIGGIN

Magnet Quartet

Chunky glitter embellishments add shine to these Native American–inspired pieces of refrigerator art.

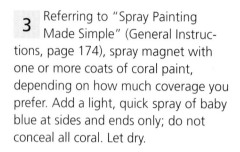

Designs by Judi Kauffman

Native American textiles, embroidery, woodcarving and American patchwork inspired this magnet quartet.

—Judy Kauffman

Materials
- Assorted wooden cutouts including 4 large squares, 8 medium squares, 8 teardrop shapes
- Quick-setting glue
- ⅛-inch double-stick tape
- Bright yellow ultrafine and flake glitter
- Spray paints: coral, baby blue
- Spiral stickers
- Fine-point paint markers: white, hot purple, black
- ½-inch round magnets

Instructions

1 For each magnet, glue together one large square, two medium squares and two teardrop cutouts, referring to photo.

2 Varying the centers, layer and glue a large shape with one or more smaller ones for each magnet.

3 Referring to "Spray Painting Made Simple" (General Instructions, page 174), spray magnet with one or more coats of coral paint, depending on how much coverage you prefer. Add a light, quick spray of baby blue at sides and ends only; do not conceal all coral. Let dry.

4 Referring to "Save That Glitter!" (General Instructions, page 174), place a strip of double-stick tape down center of each teardrop cutout and sprinkle with ultrafine glitter; shake off excess.

5 Apply glue to center shape; coat with flake glitter. Shake off excess. On magnet with heart center add more flake glitter below the triangle.

6 Closely trim spiral stickers; apply two to each magnet.

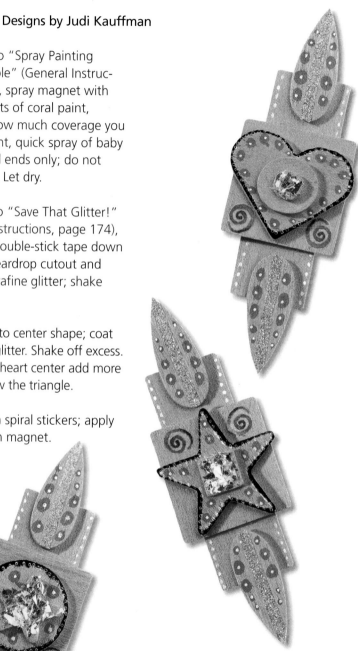

7 Outline large center shape with black paint marker. Add hot purple and white dots as desired.

8 Glue round magnet to back of each magnet. ◆

Art Deco Brooches

Simple shapes are combined with bright colors and stickers to create wearable works of art.

Designs by Mary Lynn Maloney

" I spread out a bunch of wooden shapes on my work table, then scrambled them together just to consider possible combinations that might be a bit unexpected. Layering the different shapes and sizes was fun, and after some time I had to make myself stop because the combinations seemed endless! I like the graphic, almost architectural look of these brooches. "

—**Mary Lynn Maloney**

Materials

Art Deco Brooch
- Wooden circle cutouts: 2½-inch, 1¼-inch, ¾-inch and ⅜-inch diameters
- Spray paint: yellow, light blue
- Gold/bronze glitter
- Border strip stickers: light blue, pale yellow
- Copper-leafing pen
- Craft knife
- Metal-edge ruler
- Fine-grit sandpaper
- Tack cloth

Candy Pink Brooch
- Wooden cutouts: 1½-inch square, ¾-inch and ⅜-inch circles, 2 (1½-inch) base triangles
- Spray paint: yellow, bright pink
- Fuchsia glitter
- Neon green/pink border strip sticker

Mod Retro Brooch
- Wooden cutouts: 2⅝-inch oval, 1-inch square, ¾-inch circle, 3 (⅜-inch) circles
- Spray paint: purple, coral
- Black chunky glitter
- Retro shapes/lines border strip sticker
- Craft knife

Each Brooch
- Tacky craft glue
- Satin varnish
- Felt scrap
- Paintbrush
- Pin back

Art Deco Brooch

1 Using craft knife and ruler, cut 2½-inch circle in half; cut one half in half to obtain a quarter-circle shape. Sand rough edges; wipe off dust with tack cloth.

2 Referring to "Spray Painting Made Simple" (General Instructions, page 174), spray quarter-circle with four to six light coats of yellow; in same fashion, spray 1¼-inch circle light blue.

3 Brush half-circle and ¾-inch circle with varnish; let dry.

4 Referring to "Save That Glitter" (General Instructions, page 174), brush tacky craft glue onto ⅜-inch circle, and along rounded edge of half-circle

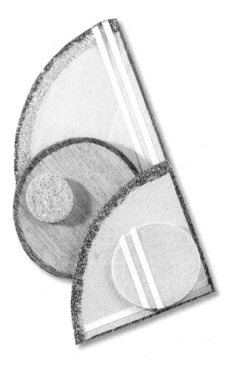

and quarter-circle; sprinkle with glitter. Shake off excess and let shapes dry.

5 Referring to photo throughout, adhere light blue sticker along straight edge of half-circle, along bottom edge of yellow quarter-circle, and slightly off-center on ¾-inch circle, folding ends of stickers around to back; press and rub stickers to secure. Repeat process with light yellow

Continued on page 23

Garden Creatures Button Covers

Transform an ordinary garment into a piece for an extra-special occasion by creating wearable accents using stickers you have on hand.

Designs by Vicki Schreiner

"Bugs buzzing around fancy-free always fascinate me. For that reason, I'm very drawn to wearables with bug designs. What better place to find little bugsies than on little Woodsies?"

—Vicki Schreiner

Materials

- Assorted wooden cutouts in "square and diamond" shapes
- Satin-finish spray paints: white, sage
- Clear stickers: bugs, butterflies, leaves
- Ultrafine glitter
- Glass and metal cement
- 17mm button covers
- Satin-finish interior varnish
- Masking tape
- Paintbrush
- Foam plates

Create

Bug stickers are fun and make great accents to coordinate with casual outfits. For dressier clothing, substitute transparent vellum flower stickers and subdued glitter colors. Make a matching pin using the same technique!

Instructions

1 Use square wooden cutout as bottom piece for each button cover. Choose a triangle or square as top of each cover.

2 Choose which side of wooden piece will be front; place loop of masking tape on this side. (See "Spray Painting Made Simple" in the General Instructions, page 174.) Stick all squares for bottom pieces onto a piece of newspaper. Spray with sage; let dry. Stick all shapes for tops on another sheet of newspaper. Spray with white; let dry. Move masking tape loops to painted side of each piece; paint backs of pieces to match fronts. Let dry.

3 Place sticker on front of each top piece as desired, allowing certain areas of sticker to overhang piece; trim excess with scissors.

4 Place about a tablespoon of glitter on a foam plate. Apply one coat of varnish to front of each green bottom piece; place piece facedown in glitter and press lightly. Turn right side up and set aside until dry.

5 Place a small pool of varnish on a foam plate. Pour some glitter into varnish and mix with paintbrush handle. Apply two coats of

mixture to front of each white top piece, coating stickers. Let dry.

6 Using cement, glue each top to a bottom; let dry completely. Apply a coat of varnish to sides and front of each piece, coating all glitter and stickers; let dry. Repeat.

7 Use cement to attach a button cover to the back of each piece. ◆

Nature Mosaic Table

Create the look of mosaic tiles with wooden pieces and dimensional lacquer.

Design by June Fiechter

" I had a table in need of a face-lift, and I wondered if Woodsies shapes could somehow look like tiles. At first I was concerned about how to incorporate the glitter and stickers, but while checking out the available sticker selections, I realized I could make something really cool. The 3-D lacquer pulls everything together.

—June Fiechter

Materials
- Table with flat wooden top
- Enough wooden cutouts to cover tabletop
- Assorted stickers
- Ultrafine glitter
- Black spray paint
- White acrylic paint
- Wood glue
- Sponge brush
- 3-D lacquer: yellow, green, light blue, aqua, clear
- Matte-finish clear glue
- Wood sealer

Instructions

1 Arrange wooden cutouts on top of table; secure with wood glue.

2 Paint top of table, including cutouts, with several coats of sealer; let dry completely.

3 Referring to "Spray Painting Made Simple" (General Instructions, page 174), spray tabletop with several coats of black paint.

4 Using sponge brush and a dabbing motion, apply two coats white paint to cutouts only, letting paint dry between coats. Before second coat dries, sprinkle glitter into the palm of your hand and blow it over the wet paint. Let dry.

5 Squeeze matte-finish clear glue onto tabletop between wooden cutouts; let dry.

6 Randomly apply stickers to wooden cutouts.

Create Try substituting different sizes of round Woodsies in place of the squares and rectangles for a totally different look. You can also use this technique to embellish a larger table, a photo frame or a garden bench.

7 Squeeze 3-D lacquer onto top of each cutout, using clear on cutouts with stickers and assorted colors as desired on other cutouts. Let dry. ◆

Glitter-Girl Photo Box

A border of fringy fiber adds fun to a useful storage box.

Design by Katie Hacker

Materials
- 7¾ x 11¾-inch pink photo box
- 4 (⅞-inch-wide) multicolored heart stickers
- Alphabet stickers to spell "photos"
- Wooden cutouts: 4 (⅜-inch) circles, 4 (1¼-inch) circles, 4 (1½-inch) squares
- Paper or card-stock rectangles: 4½ x 5-inch and 7¼ x 10¾-inch black, 4¾ x 5¼-inch white
- Ultrafine glitter: pink, blue, green, yellow, orange
- Silver spray paint
- Clear acrylic spray sealer
- 39-inch piece 1½-inch-wide coordinating decorative trim
- Glue stick
- Craft glue
- Heavy book

Instructions

1 Place 1¼-inch wooden circles on wooden squares; trace around circles with pencils. Remove circles. Referring to "Spray Painting Made Simple" (General Instructions, page 174), spray circles with silver paint; set aside to dry.

2 Referring to "Save That Glitter!" (General Instructions, page 174), spread even layer of craft glue on one square outside circle outline and sprinkle with yellow glitter. Shake off excess.

In same fashion, apply orange, pink and green glitter to remaining squares. Spray squares with sealer; let dry.

3 Position heart sticker in center of each silver circle; use craft glue to affix a silver stickered circle to each glittered square.

4 Spread thin border of craft glue ¼ inch wide around edge of white paper or card stock and sprinkle with blue glitter. Shake off excess. Spray glittered area with sealer; let dry.

5 Using glue stick, glue larger black rectangle in center of top of photo box; glue glittered white rectangle 2 inches from top edge of box. Glue smaller black rectangle centered on white rectangle. Lay

heavy book on photo box lid; let dry.

6 Glue glittered squares to center black rectangle, positioning them ¾ inch from top and bottom edges and ½ inch from side edges of black rectangle.

7 Spread thin layer of craft glue over ⅜-inch circles and sprinkle with pink glitter. Shake off excess; let dry. Spray pink circles with sealer; let dry. When dry, glue one in each corner of larger black rectangle.

8 Trim alphabet stickers to leave ⅛-inch border around letters. Spread thin layer of glue over each letter and sprinkle each with a different color of glitter. While glue is still wet, carefully peel stickers from backing

and press into place on top of box. (If you wait until glue dries, it may be too difficult to peel stickers from backing.)

9 Glue decorative trim around edge of box lid. Spread glue over label holder on front of box; sprinkle blue glitter onto label holder. ◆

"These island-inspired glitters remind me of the spectacular sunsets in the Florida Keys. I wanted the glitters to be the focus for this fun and functional project, and I just happened to have coordinating stickers and trim. The same design would look great in other color schemes, depending on what supplies you have in your craft closet.

—Katie Hacker

Art Deco Brooches
Continued from page 19

sticker, adhering it along blue sticker on half-circle and ¾-inch circle.

6 Run copper-leafing pen along edges of half-circle, blue circle and yellow quarter-circle.

7 Glue pieces together. Cut felt to size and shape for backing; glue to back of assembled pin. Glue pin back to felt.

Candy Pink Brooch

1 Referring to "Spray Painting Made Simple" (General Instructions, page 174), spray ¾-inch circle with four to six light coats of yellow; in same fashion, spray ⅜-inch circle and one triangle bright pink.

2 Adhere sticker along top edge of square, folding ends of sticker around to back; press and rub sticker to secure. Referring to photo

throughout, adhere sticker to unpainted triangle at an angle. Brush both shapes with varnish; let dry.

3 Brush pink circle and pink triangle with varnish; let dry.

4 Referring to "Save That Glitter!" (General Instructions, page 174), brush tacky craft glue onto left and right side edges of square and sprinkle with glitter; shake off excess and let shapes dry.

5 Glue pieces together. Cut felt to size and shape for backing; glue to back of assembled pin. Glue pin back to felt.

Mod Retro Brooch

1 Referring to "Spray Painting Made Simple" (General Instructions, page 174), spray ¾-inch circle with four to six light coats of coral;

in same fashion, spray oval and three ⅜-inch circles purple.

2 Adhere sticker along center of oval; using craft knife, carefully trim sticker around edges of oval. Press and rub sticker to secure.

3 Brush oval and three purple circles with varnish; let dry.

4 Referring to "Save That Glitter!" (General Instructions, page 174), brush tacky craft glue along left and right side edges of square and sprinkle with glitter. Shake off excess and let shapes dry.

5 Referring to photo throughout, glue pieces together. Cut felt to size and shape for backing; glue to back of assembled pin. Glue pin back to felt. ◆

Contemporary Shadow Box

A hint of glitter adds sparkle and dimension to the simple shapes and colorful flower stickers.

Design by Lisa Galvin

Materials
- 8⅛-inch-square, 1½-inch-deep shadow-box frame
- Satin-finish spray paint: eggshell white, periwinkle blue, freesia, kiwi green
- 6 x 3½-inch piece Plexiglas
- Wooden cutouts: 3 large squares, 3 medium squares, 3 small squares, 24 small circles
- Art glitter: purple, rose, green
- Vellum flower stickers with leaves
- Fine-grit sandpaper
- Tack cloth
- Drop cloth
- Self-adhesive vinyl shelf-lining paper
- Tacky glue
- Clear gem glue
- Foam plate
- Straight pin
- Scrap paper
- Glass cleaner
- Paper towel *or* lint-free cloth
- Picture hanger
- Hammer

Use this technique to showcase the large variety of vellum stickers available today. Different colors and shapes of wooden pieces can change the look from contemporary to something a little more traditional.

Create

Hints & Helps

Hold wooden cutouts in place for painting: Peel paper backing from appropriate-size piece of shelf-lining paper; place adhesive side up on flat surface covered with drop cloth. Tape corners to hold. Place cutouts on adhesive, leaving at least 15 inches between separate colors being sprayed to keep one color from corrupting another.

Touch-ups: To touch up missed areas, scratches or "goofs" from smeared glue and other mishaps that can occur while working on spray-painted projects, spray a puddle of matching color onto a foam plate, etc., and use an old paintbrush to apply paint.

Plexiglas can be purchased and cut to size at most hardware and home improvement stores. Sand rough-cut edges with fine-grit sandpaper. To avoid scratches, do not remove protective plastic film until ready to use or mount Plexiglas.

Instructions

1. Sand frame to remove rough edges and surfaces; remove dust with tack cloth. Refer to "Spray Painting Made Simple" (General Instructions, page 174). Place frame on drop cloth; spray with eggshell white; let dry. Repeat to add three or four even, light coats. Turn over and repeat to paint opposite side.

2. *Spacers:* Glue together wooden circles to make four stacks of five circles each; let dry. Stand upright on adhesive-backed shelf liner and spray with eggshell white.

3. Spray-paint one of each size square with periwinkle blue, freesia and kiwi green; paint remaining four circles periwinkle blue; let dry. Repeat to add three or four even, light coats.

4. Referring to photo throughout, use tacky glue to assemble three sets of squares as shown. Add glitter accents by pouring a small amount of glue onto foam plate; one piece at a time, use straight pin to apply thin lines and dots of glue to stickers and squares in areas you choose to highlight. Referring to "Save That Glitter!" (General Instructions, page 174), pour on coordinating color of glitter; shake off excess and let dry. Repeat as needed, working with one color of glitter at a time.

5. Attach hanger to back of frame.

6. *Assemble shadow box:* Glue square sets at top. Determine positions of circular "spacers" at corners of Plexiglas; they will hold Plexiglas up off frame. Use ruler and pencil to measure, then mark a dot inside frame, matching spacer placement on Plexiglas. Glue spacers inside frame, covering marked dots. Let dry. Apply flower stickers inside frame.

7. Lightly sand edges of Plexiglas; remove protective plastic film from both sides. Clean Plexiglas with glass cleaner and paper towel.

8 Apply gem glue to top of each spacer; set Plexiglas into frame on spacers, over flower stickers and flush with bottom. Adhere periwinkle blue circles on top of Plexiglas to cover ends of spacers; let dry. Apply leaf stickers to Plexiglas, arranging them between and around flowers. ◆

" I love working with Woodsies and spray-painting them for quick, even coverage is a breeze! Stickers were a new design element for me, and I was pleasantly surprised by the quality and styles available. The hardest part of the whole project was choosing which stickers I wanted to use and which ones I had to put back on the rack—I wanted them all! "

—**Lisa Galvin**

BEADS
Pigment Powders
Fibers
Paper Clay
WIRE

These materials are all hot crafting commodities, so you're sure to have them in your craft closet. Feel free to substitute small beads for larger ones, fuzzy fibers for metallic, or whatever you may have on hand. It's all about the creativity!

Craft Closet Challenge
Bluebird Box

The challenge—each designer needs to create a project using the materials we selected (and one or two more items they add).

Design by June Fiechter

Materials
- Provo Craft glass jewelry box
- Glass paints: blue, light blue
- Artistic Wire color-coated wire in two complementary shades of blue
- Assorted Blue Moon beads from Elizabeth Ward & Co.
- Adornments decorative fibers from EK Success
- Delight modeling medium from Creative Paperclay
- Small bird foam stamp
- Pearl-Ex sparkle gold powdered pigment from Jacquard
- Needle-nose pliers
- Glue

Instructions

1 Referring to photo throughout, apply light blue paint to horizontal glass surface. While still wet, drop on beads. Allow paint to dry. (Sample was set in front of a fan while paint dried, producing the crackled effect.)

2 Repeat on other surfaces of box until all surfaces are covered with paint and beads. When doing top of lid, position a single bead in each corner.

3 Referring to Fig. 1 and using needle-nose pliers, curl wires into a total of three

Fig. 1

different ornaments. Attach a bead to the top of each and set ornaments aside.

4 Roll paper-based clay ¼ inch thick. Gently press stamp into clay. Remove stamp and insert coiled wires through clay above head. Allow clay to harden slightly. If desired, press additional beads into the stamped clay image at this point, before it hardens.

5 Trim away excess clay from around image. Reshape and smooth edges of clay.

6 Lay clay image flat and fill indentations in design with blue glass paint. Let dry.

7 Mix sparkle gold powdered pigment with a little glue, and paint clay piece with mixture; let dry.

8 Glue clay piece to box lid; let glue dry.

9 Cut a piece of fiber and tie in a bow, leaving long tails. Glue bow to front of box at top. Trim ends to equal length; glue ends to box beside bow. ◆

There are a million things you can do with paper-based clay. Stamping it is one of my favorites. I opted to go with blue glass paint, and thus decided on a bluebird. This is a super-simple project—just be patient with the drying time.

—June Fiechter

Craft Closet Challenge
Asian Serenity Box

Design by Judi Kauffman

Materials
- Provo Craft glass jewelry box
- Artistic Wire purple 22-gauge silver-plated copper wire
- Blue Moon purple *and* pink frosted round *and* square glass beads from Elizabeth Ward & Co.
- Adornments Pansies #AD30010 decorative fibers from EK Success
- Mauve Delight modeling medium from Creative Paperclay
- Asian Expression rubber stamps from Red Castle: Asian-style fan *and* calligraphy motifs
- Pearl-Ex powdered pigments from Jacquard: duo green-yellow, super copper
- Gloss-finish acrylic medium
- Paintbrush
- 7 x 9-inch remnant silk fabric
- 3½ x 5½-inch rectangle cardboard
- Craft batting *or* tissues
- Glue
- Paper clip
- Rolling pin

Instructions

1 Roll golf ball-size lump of paper-based clay ¼ inch thick. Press fan rubber stamp onto clay; cut out with craft knife. Open a paper clip; press end repeatedly into top edge of fan to give it a lacy appearance.

2 Roll three balls of clay each the size of a grape; press to flatten. Press the calligraphy rubber stamp

several times onto each clay circle. Roll circles into oval tubes, pinching edges of clay together at back to seal; let all clay pieces dry.

3 *For each leg of box:* Thread 10 round frosted glass beads onto a piece of purple wire and twist ends together to make a tiny "bracelet." Secure a bracelet around each leg, cutting off excess wire.

4 *Cushion:* Cover cardboard with batting (or a smooth stack of tissues). Pull fabric over edges of

cardboard to cover batting; glue fabric edges to back of cardboard. Beginning and ending on back, wind three strands of fine decorative fiber lengthwise over cushion, gluing ends to back. Wind five strands of the same fiber widthwise over cushion to form a grid.

5 Mix duo green-yellow pigment with gloss medium to the consistency of sour cream. Paint clay pieces with mixture; let dry.

6 Mix super copper pigment with gloss medium to same consistency. Using very little of the mixture, brush just the surface of the clay pieces to highlight details; let dry.

7 Referring to photo throughout, add fibers to wide end of one clay bead and wire to end of the other two. Add wire and frosted glass beads to one end of the fan. Add more beads and wire to complete the collage as desired. Glue all elements to cushion. Clean glass and put cushion with collage inside box. ◆

This challenge was a difficult one. I liked the box so much plain that I felt anything I added would ruin it. Then I remembered a beautiful glass vitrine I had seen on a trip to Paris—and realized that I could create a serene, miniature world inside the box.

The French word vitrine applies to both a display case and a window. To tone down the metal a bit, I used frosted glass beads and wire to make elegant little bracelets for the legs. I found a piece of silk to coordinate with the finest-scale fiber in the assortment for the cushion. Then I made the collage and glued it in place.

It would be fun to leave the pieces loose. That way, the collage could be changed with each season or holiday.

—**Judi Kauffman**

Craft Closet Challenge
Celtic Trinket Box

Design by Mary Lynn Maloney

Materials
- Provo Craft glass jewelry box
- Artistic Wire 22-gauge silver-plated copper wire: tangerine, gold
- Blue Moon mixed red glass mini beads from Elizabeth Ward & Co.
- Adornments assorted red decorative fibers from EK Success
- Delight modeling medium from Creative Paperclay
- Celtic-design push mold
- Highlander Celtic Stamps Celtic spiral rubber stamp
- Pearl-Ex powdered pigments from Jacquard: sparkle gold, super copper, antique silver, duo green-yellow
- Matte spray sealer
- Paintbrush
- Gem glue
- Clear-drying craft glue
- Large paper clip
- Rolling pin
- Wire cutters

Instructions

1 Roll 2-inch ball of paper-based clay to an irregular shape approximately 2½ x 4 inches. Randomly press uninked spiral rubber stamp onto clay. Open paper clip; use end to pierce the clay six to eight times randomly around edge (wire will be threaded through these holes later).

2 Press 1-inch ball of clay firmly into the two triangle shapes in the push mold. Release clay onto smooth work surface; trim shapes with craft knife. Repeat to make two more triangles.

3 Press 2-inch ball of clay into the rectangular repeated Celtic knot shape in the push mold. Release clay; trim with knife. Let all clay shapes air-dry for 24 hours.

4 Mix 2 tablespoons glue with 2 teaspoons sparkle gold powdered pigment. Paint dried molded shapes with two coats of mixture, letting it dry between coats.

5 Mix 2 tablespoons glue with 2 teaspoons super copper powdered pigment. Paint dried stamped spiral shape with two coats of mixture, letting it dry between coats.

6 Using a dry paintbrush, randomly brush Celtic shapes with dry powdered pigment in this order: antique silver, super copper, duo green-yellow. Spray pieces with matte sealer.

7 Brush copper-painted clay piece with dry duo green-yellow pigment. Spray with matte sealer.

8 Cut 2 yards red decorative fiber. Apply dots of gem glue to upper edge of glass box just below rim. Wrap fiber twice around box, pressing it into glue to secure.

9 Using gem glue, glue Celtic triangles onto corners of box's lid. Glue long, rectangular Celtic shape onto center of stamped clay shape.

10 Cut a 22-inch piece of tangerine wire. Carefully thread and wrap wire through holes punched in copper clay piece and over the Celtic clay piece. As you wrap, thread beads onto the wire and add small coils and loops with wire snips.

11 Cut 12-inch lengths of each of two different red fibers and tangerine and gold wires. Gather wires and fibers and twist ends together, leaving about 2 inches at both ends. Add two or three beads to ends of wires and secure by making small coils in wire with wire snips.

12 Lay assembled fiber/wire piece made in step 11 across top of glass box. Apply a generous amount of gem glue to back of assembled clay/wire piece (step 10) and glue to center of lid over fiber/wire piece. Add dots of gem glue under ends of fiber/wire piece to secure. Let dry, carefully adding weight if necessary. ◆

"This glass box is so smooth and sleek; it just called out for some contrasting texture. The molded clay, fibers and beads are great for texture and add a nice, warm, metallic color as well.
—Mary Lynn Maloney

Polka-Dot Treasure Box

Dots and swirls abound on this fun box that will become a treasure holder for your favorite young girl!

Design by Chris Malone

Materials

- 6¼-inch square wooden box with hinged lid and ball-knob feet
- Paper-based air-drying clay
- 1-inch wooden bead
- Assorted fibers for tassel: yarn, metallic cords, pearl cotton, narrow ribbon, etc.
- Assorted glass, plastic and/or metallic beads for tassel
- 8 metallic green ³⁄₁₆- to ¼-inch beads for flower centers
- 60 inches 18-gauge metallic green wire
- Powdered pigments: duo green-yellow, macro pearl, antique bronze
- Acrylic craft paints: sky blue, white, golden brown, lime green, bright yellow, pink
- Spray matte finish
- 4 small photos
- Waxed paper or plastic wrap
- Rolling pin
- Knife
- Paintbrush
- ½-inch foam stencil dauber or ½-inch circle cut from compressed sponge
- Glue

Instructions

1 Roll paper-based clay ¼ inch thick between two sheets of waxed paper or plastic wrap. Referring to pattern (page 32), use sharp knife to cut four frames from rolled clay. Smooth edges with finger dipped in water. (Shapes can be somewhat irregular.)

2 Roll a portion of leftover clay ⅛ inch thick. Referring to pattern, cut 16 leaves. Using blunt edge of knife, indent shallow vein down center of each.

3 Form five ¼-inch balls of clay; place on waxed paper in circle to form flower. Wet sides of balls where they touch to "glue" them together; then press down on all balls evenly to form a five-petal flower. Repeat to make a total of eight flowers.

4 Dry frames, leaves and flowers following manufacturer's instructions. If petals separate, reattach with a dot of glue.

5 Paint frames golden brown, leaves lime green and flowers white. Let dry.

6 Using paintbrush or finger, rub powdered pigments onto shapes: antique bronze on frames, duo green-yellow on leaves and macro pearl on flowers. **Note:** *It is not necessary to completely cover painted pieces with pigment.*

7 Referring to directions for base-coating under Painting Techniques in the General Instructions (page 174), base-coat box and lid with blue, top knob with yellow, and feet and

Beads, wire and fibers seem a natural combination for embellishing almost anything, but including the paper-based clay made it possible to add another element. I wanted to keep it simple, and I love dimensional decorations, so I chose to make small frames with flowers and leaves. The flowers are cheerful, so I chose a bright and happy color scheme for the paints and fibers.

—Chris Malone

bead for tassel with pink. Add a second coat as needed. Paint tiny white dots around center of tassel bead. Dip dauber into white and touch to box; repeat to randomly cover blue portions of box and lid with dots, reapplying paint before stamping each. Let all paints dry.

8 Spray all wood and clay pieces with two light coats of matte finish, letting it dry between coats. If desired, touch up clay pieces with additional powdered pigment.

9 Cut four photos to fit frames; glue to frames. Glue a flower on two opposite corners of each frame; glue two leaves around each flower. Glue one frame in center on each side of box.

10 *Tassel:* Cut assorted fibers in 10-inch lengths, cutting sufficient fibers so that when doubled, they fit snugly inside bead. Wrap cord around center of bundle; knot ends and clip off excess. Cut 12-inch cord and slip under tying cord on tassel. Tie a knot near the ends of the cord. Push cord through bead and pull to bring top of tassel ⅜ inch out other side of bead. Wrap cord around knob on top of lid and push tassel through cord loop; pull tight.

11 From wire, cut one piece 36 inches and one piece 48 inches long. Start a tight coil at one end of shorter piece; using your fingers, continue to shape wire into irregular concentric circles until almost half of wire is used. Repeat from other end. Wrap center of wire around knob on top of lid and twist ends together once to hold. Repeat with longer wire, but wrap it around knob twice and bring one coil down over front of box. Arrange coils so that they do not overlap. Slip additional photos or other memorabilia into coils for display. ◆

Leaf   **Treasure Box Frame**

Aztec-Influence Decorative Box

Vary the theme of your box by choosing a favorite stamp motif and color scheme.

Design by Judi Kauffman

Create

Instead of using a stamp, emboss the paper-based clay motif with natural leaves and sticks before highlighting with pearlescent colors. Adapt Judi's shell suggestion and add dried leaves and sticks around the side of the lid.

" I love to walk barefoot on the beach, collecting shells and stones, so I thought it would be fun to make a treasure box to hold them. For my two additional supplies I chose black paint and rubber stamps, but I might glue some shells along the sides of the lid when I get the box back. Just because we designers have "rules" to follow doesn't mean that you do! "

—Judi Kauffman

Materials
- Papier-mâché or cardboard box with lid
- 22-gauge turquoise silver-plated copper wire
- 11 tiny black iris flower beads
- Paper-based air-drying clay
- Rubber stamps: 4-inch fish, ½-inch circle
- Powdered pigments: duo green/yellow, super copper
- Black acrylic craft paint
- Gloss-finish acrylic medium
- Paintbrush
- Glue
- Sponge

Instructions

1 Flatten package of clay into a ½-inch-thick rectangle. Press large fish rubber stamp into center of clay. Press circle stamp randomly into clay around fish. Referring to photo throughout, use end of paintbrush to create a pattern around the edges of the fish and the clay panel itself, pressing handle tip straight into the clay to make holes or dots, or pressing it in on its side to make ridges. Let clay dry.

2 Paint box black; let dry.

3 Mix green/yellow powdered pigment with gloss medium to the consistency of sour cream. Sponge mixture onto box and sides of lid. Using an almost-dry brush, paint dry clay panel with same mixture, allowing some white clay to show.

4 Mix super copper powder and medium to same consistency and brush mixture onto surface of clay to add richer tones of color, allowing some green/yellow and plain white clay to show through. Using almost-dry brush, brush a tiny amount of black acrylic paint onto the clay for a "smoky" effect.

5 Glue beads onto clay.

6 Twist wire to spell name or greeting; twist another piece to make random swirls. Position wire and clay panel on top of box lid and glue in place, concealing ends of wire under clay panel. ◆

Looks-Great-With-Denim Necklace

Your silk suit will be jealous of the necklace you only wear with your favorite jeans!

Design by Katie Hacker

Materials

- Paper-based air-drying clay
- 48 inches blue fuzzy yarn
- 22-gauge silver craft wire
- 18 inches flexible beading wire
- Powdered pigments: blue, purple
- Clear acrylic spray sealer
- Round matte glass beads: 8 (7mm) blue, 6 (6mm) dark pink, 4 (8mm) light pink
- 14 silver "dotted" spacer beads
- 6 silver "braided" spacer beads
- Silver lobster clasp and tag
- 2 silver crimp beads (see Project Note)
- 4mm mandrel (or chopstick or knitting needle)
- Bamboo skewer
- Chain-nose pliers
- Craft glue

The inspiration for this necklace came from my favorite denim jacket. Handmade yarn and wire beads, paper-based clay beads and purchased matte glass beads produce the perfect balance of softness and shine. It's comfortable but spunky, just like my favorite jacket.

—Katie Hacker

Project Note

You may choose to use special crimping pliers that make the crimp beads round instead of flat when squeezed. If you choose not to use crimp beads, purchase flexible beading wire that is easy to knot. Secure all knots with a drop of super glue.

Instructions

1. Form three ½-inch balls from paper-based clay. Press skewer

Continued on page 41

Paper Roses Potpourri Ball

This pretty, feminine indulgence is created with soft fibers and elegant "paper roses" created from no-bake clay.

Design by Lorine Mason

"I have always loved forming flowers from clay. The roses I created for the top of this potpourri ball are a perfect fit with the rose-petal potpourri that I discovered at my local craft store. The fiber, wire and bead embellishments are just for fun!"
—**Lorine Mason**

Materials
- Paper-based air-drying clay
- Miniature leaf cookie cutters
- Toothpick
- Acrylic craft paints in desired colors for roses and leaves
- Gold powdered pigment
- Plastic refillable potpourri ball
- Rose-petal potpourri
- Assorted fibers: ribbon, yarn, embroidery thread
- Heart-shape beads: 1 large, 4 small
- Gold craft wire
- Paintbrush
- Rolling pin
- Cardboard
- Pencil *or* slender dowel rod
- Hot-glue gun

Instructions

1 *Sculpt individual rose petals from paper-based clay:* Pinch a ¼-inch ball of clay between your thumb and index finger to make a teardrop shape, taking the time to thin the edges. Make at least four petals for the smallest flower, up to nine for the largest roses.

2 *Form center of rose:* Tightly roll a single petal shape. Add petals around rose center, slightly overlapping each and flaring edges slightly outward. As each row of petals is added, move down the rolled center to achieve a balanced look. Continue adding petals until rose is desired size. Pinch excess clay off bottom.

3 Form rosebuds from two or three tightly rolled petals, curving only the last petal's edge slightly outward.

4 Cut leaves from flattened clay with cookie cutters; create veins using a toothpick. Let dry.

5 Add water to acrylic paint and, using paintbrush, apply a wash of color to leaves and roses. Dip wet brush into pigment and brush over tops of roses and leaves; let dry.

6 Fill potpourri ball with potpourri. Referring to photo throughout, wrap circumference of ball six or eight times with fibers, starting at the top and crossing around the hanging loop each time. Glue ends neatly.

7 *Tassel:* Wrap a combination of fibers around a 3-inch piece of cardboard. Thread a length of yarn through one end of the wrapped fibers; knot it. Slide loop of fibers off cardboard. Wrap a piece of yarn, ribbon or thread several times around fibers ½ inch from the first knot; glue neatly. Cut through fibers at bottom of loop; fluff and trim ends of tassel. Hot-glue tassel to bottom of potpourri ball; hot-glue large bead to top of tassel.

8 Wrap pieces of wire around pencil or slender dowel rod to create spirals. Slide coils off; add small bead(s) to one end of some of the spirals.

9 Thread 8-inch piece of ribbon through hanging loop at top of the potpourri ball; knot ends together. Hot-glue roses, leaves and wire spirals to top of potpourri ball as desired. ◆

Floral Memory Book

Create a delicate look or go bold and bright, simply by changing the embellishments on the cover of this journal.

Design by Mary Ayres

Materials
- 6 x 8-inch journal
- 2 coordinating patterned papers
- 4 coordinating fibers: fuzzy, wide, medium and a narrow thread
- Spool of gold wire
- 5mm white pearl beads
- Paper-based air-drying clay
- Gold powdered pigment
- Square rubber stamp
- Small paintbrush
- Needle-nose pliers
- Glue pen for paper
- Fabric glue
- White craft glue
- Deckle-edge scissors

Project Note
Adjust measurements as needed if you use a different-size journal.

Instructions

1 Cut a 6½ x 4¾-inch rectangle from one paper; using glue pen, glue to top right side of journal cover. Cut a 6½ x 1¼-inch rectangle from second paper; glue to bottom right side of cover. Round corners of paper rectangles with scissors so they are even with corners of journal.

2 Glue wide fiber horizontally across journal cover to separate papers; glue end on right side inside cover. Glue medium fiber on top of wide fiber's edges, twisting fiber to give it more texture; glue ends on right side inside cover. Wrap and glue wide fiber vertically around empty space on left side of cover, covering edges of paper and fiber; glue ends inside cover. Wrap and glue medium fiber vertically around wide fiber, covering edges, twisting fiber and gluing ends inside cover.

3 Use pliers to bend end of wire in a small loop; using pliers, continue to bend wire back and forth until length measures 6 inches. Cut wire from spool and bend remaining end in a small loop.

4 Knot one end of fuzzy fiber; thread fiber in and out through bends in wire, keeping it straight. Knot fiber at end of wire and trim off excess.

5 Attach thread to one end of wire. String beads onto thread as you weave thread in and out of wire, following the fuzzy fiber. Knot thread at end of wire. Glue assembled wire/fiber embellishment to right side of vertical fibers on cover.

6 Roll paper clay ¼ inch thick. Press stamp into clay, then lift straight up. Trim edges with decorative scissors. Let clay shape air-dry.

7 Brush glue on top edges of clay shape, then rub powdered pigment on top of glue. Glue shape on the diagonal to center of paper at top of journal. Glue medium fiber around edge of paper-clay shape, twisting fiber. Brush glue on design details on paper and rub powdered pigment on glue; wipe off excess powder.

8 Cut rectangle from patterned paper slightly smaller than cover; glue inside cover to hide fiber ends. ◆

I was inspired to make the journal by the beautiful toile paper that I purchased in a scrapbooking store. I gathered the other elements that matched the paper, including the flower paper, green fibers, gold wire, and pearl beads. All of the additional items added interesting textures to the completed design. I kept working with the elements that I had chosen until I came up with a pleasing design.

—Mary Ayres

Tag Trio

Tag art is all the rage in crafts, and these tags are
a good example of what you can create with scraps
of card stock and leftover paper-based clay.

Designs by Samantha McNesby

Materials

Peace Tag
- Paper-based air-drying clay
- Powdered pigments: pale green, black, bright pink
- 8 (12-inch) strands assorted yarn or other fibers
- 3 (6-inch) fiber scraps
- Scraps of red 24-gauge wire
- 6 (¼-inch) gold spacer beads
- Scrabble tiles to spell "PEACE"
- Homemade or purchased red paper tag
- Thick white craft glue or hot-glue gun
- 1-inch scruffy paintbrush
- Eyedropper

Wire Heart Tag
- Paper-based air-drying clay
- Powdered pigments: bright pink, black
- 4 (12-inch) strands assorted yarn or other fibers
- 6-inch piece black 16- or 18-gauge wire
- Spacer beads: 4 (⅜-inch) floral

glass, 1 (¼-inch) silver
- 2 (4mm or 6mm) round silver beads
- Scrap of taupe or ivory paper
- Homemade or purchased red paper tag
- Thick white craft glue or hot-glue gun
- 1-inch scruffy paintbrush
- Deckle-edge scissors

Medallions Tag
- Paper-based air-drying clay
- Small medallion-shape push mold (optional)
- Powdered pigments: black, bright pink
- 5 (12-inch) strands hemp fiber
- Black 28-gauge wire
- 8 assorted ⅜- to ½-inch glass beads
- Scrap of red paper
- Thick white craft glue or hot-glue gun
- 1-inch scruffy paintbrush
- Eyedropper
- Tapestry needle

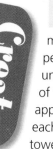

These tags can have a totally different look depending on the beads and fibers you select. Use whatever you have on hand to coordinate with specialty card stocks and wires.

Peace Tag

1 Place a small amount of pale green powdered pigment on palette. Using eyedropper, add water a drop at a time until mixture is the consistency of thin paste. Using scruffy brush, apply a coat of the mixture to each letter tile. Blot with paper towel and let dry.

2 Referring to photo throughout, use the tip of your finger to rub random streaks of pigment mixture onto the tag without covering it completely.

3 Glue three 6-inch strands of yarn across the front of the tag, laying the yarn randomly across the surface. Let dry.

4 Glue letter tiles to tag; let dry.

5 Using your fingers, mold three ½- to 1-inch cylindrical beads from paper-based clay. Using a piece of wire, poke a hole through each bead large enough to accommodate one of the fibers you are using. Use the side of the wire to impress lines around the bead. Let beads dry completely.

6 Place a small amount of black powdered pigment on palette. Again add water a drop at a time to form a thin paste. Use scruffy brush to apply a coat of pigment to beads, filling in all crevices; let dry.

7 Using the tip of your finger, apply random streaks of bright pink powdered pigment to each bead.

8 Wrap red wire around each bead.

9 Fold eight 12-inch strands of yarn in half; pass loop through hole in top of tag. Pass yarn ends

When I reviewed the list of products for the designs in this chapter, I realized I had a lot of great items on hand—but in very small quantities! I chose plain paper as the surface because I wanted the embellishments to really stand out.

I designed the tags to be displayed together by using the same color scheme for each. The tags match, even though slightly different materials were used for each.

—Samantha McNesby

through loop to secure strands in a lark's head knot.

10 Select one strand of yarn and string on one gold spacer bead, clay bead and another gold bead. Tie simple overhand knot above and below beads to hold them in place. Repeat to add beads to two more strands of yarn.

Wire Heart Tag

1 Use deckle-edge scissors to trim a piece of taupe or ivory paper to fit in center of red tag. Glue in place; let dry.

2 Referring to step 1 for Peace Tag, make a thin paste of water and bright pink powdered pigment. Referring to photo throughout, use the tip of your finger to rub random streaks of color onto the tag without covering it completely.

3 Glue a floral bead in each corner of taupe paper; let dry.

4 Fold wire in half. Using your fingers and referring to photo throughout, coil ends and fold inward to form heart shape. (It doesn't have to be perfect; it should look handmade.) Glue heart to front of tag; let dry.

5 Using your fingers, mold a 1-inch heart-shaped bead from

paper-based clay. Using a piece of wire, poke a hole through bead large enough to accommodate one of the fibers you are using. Let bead dry completely.

6 Again referring to step 1 for Peace Tag, make a thin paste of water and black powdered pigment. Using scruffy brush, apply a coat of mixture to heart bead; let dry. Use the tip of your finger to rub random streaks of bright pink powdered pigment onto heart bead without covering it completely.

7 Hold strands of yarn together and fold in half; pass loop through hole in tag. Pass yarn ends through loop to secure yarns in a lark's head knot.

8 Select one strand of yarn and string on one round silver bead, heart-shaped clay bead, silver spacer bead and another round silver bead. Tie simple overhand knot below beads to hold them in place.

Medallions Tag

1 Mold two small medallions from paper-based clay, using a push mold or just your fingers; let dry completely.

2 Referring to step 1 for Peace Tag, make a thin paste of water and

black powdered pigment. Using scruffy brush, apply a coat of the mixture to each medallion, filling all indentations. Let dry.

3 Referring to photo throughout, use the tip of your finger to rub bright pink pigment onto the face of each medallion without covering it completely.

4 Using deckle-edge scissors, trim a rectangle of red paper to fit in center of your tag. Glue paper to tag; let dry. Use the tip of your finger to rub random streaks of bright pink pigment onto the tag.

5 Using tapestry needle, poke holes through tag around edge of red rectangle, about ¼ inch from edge and ¼ inch apart. "Sew" through holes with black wire, bringing it up through one hole, down through the next, etc. Twist wire ends together on back of tag.

6 Glue medallions to tag; let dry.

7 Holding hemp strands together, fold them in half and pass them through the hole in the top of the tag. Pass the tails through the loop and tug to secure in a lark's head knot. Thread a bead onto eight of the 10 ends, knotting ends to hold beads in place. ◆

Kokopelli Candle

Add a touch of the Southwest to your home with a candle embellished with the spirit of Kokopelli.

Designs by Sharon M. Reinhart

Materials
- Ivory 3-inch-diameter pillar candle
- Kokopelli rubber stamp
- Powdered pigments: super copper, sunset gold, sparkle gold
- Stamping medium
- 20-gauge copper wire: brown, copper
- Beads: gold, copper, silver
- Paper-based air-drying clay
- Candle-painting medium
- Selected fiber
- Clear-coat spray (optional)
- Small paintbrush
- Pliers
- Acrylic roller *or* rolling pin
- Talcum powder
- Tacky craft glue
- Heat tool
- Towel
- Cosmetic foam wedge

Instructions

1 The Kokopelli image can be stamped six times around a 3-inch-diameter candle. Lay candle on a towel to keep it from rolling. Lay uninked stamp on candle as a guide, and lightly mark the bottom of the candle at the starting point of each image.

2 Ink stamp with stamping medium; place stamp rubber side up on work surface. Use a paintbrush to dab sunset gold and super copper pigments onto prepared stamp; set stamp aside.

3 Using the heat tool, heat a small area the approximate size of the Kokopelli image near the bottom of the candle, applying heat for about 10 seconds or until wax starts to soften. Then press stamp into heated area, using a rocking motion to impress stamp from one side to the other. Do not worry if some images are deeper than others; this will add depth and dimension to the piece.

Different stamps will give this candle a look to coordinate with any style of decorating. Try flower stamps with pastel colors of powdered pigment with a coordinating clay motif; brightly colored wires and beads can complete the transformation into a garden room accent.

Create

Inspiration for this project came first from the beautiful colors available in the powdered pigments and the different forms in which they can be utilized.

—Sharon M. Reinhart

4 Repeat step 3 to stamp Kokopelli images around candle; reapply pigments for each stamping, and after every second stamping, wipe stamp with a wet cloth, then reapply stamping medium and pigments. When heating candle, take care not to melt previously stamped images.

5 Mix a small amount of powdered pigment with a small amount of candle-painting medium. Using cosmetic wedge, sponge top of candle lightly with mixture. Use a paintbrush to touch up stamped images with the pigment/

medium mixture. Set candle aside.

6 Knead a small amount of paper-based clay; using a roller lightly dusted with talcum powder, roll clay to 1/8-inch thickness. Dust sparkle gold powdered pigment onto rolled clay. Dust rubber stamp with talcum, then press into clay. Remove stamp. Using a paintbrush, dab the impressed image with sunset gold and super copper powdered pigments. If desired, spray stamped image with a clear-coat sealer.

7 Lay clay piece on candle so that clay dries in the shape of the candle. Once dry, glue it to the candle with tacky craft glue as shown.

8 Cut lengths of brown and copper wire equal in measurement to the circumference of your candle *plus*

3 inches. Twist wires together loosely, holding one end with pliers.

9 Wrap twisted wire around candle, overlapping the clay medallion. Twist wires at front to secure. Unwrap wire tails from the end to just before the secured twist (wire will resemble heavy threads). Attach four beads to each wire thread, looping ends with pliers to secure.

10 Cut four 6-inch lengths of coordinating fibers. Holding them together, tie them in a knot underneath the wire where it was twisted to secure it. Trim as desired.

11 To burn candle without removing the embellishments, burn down or carve out an area large enough to insert a tea light candle. *Never leave a burning candle unattended.* ◆

Looks-Great-With-Denim Necklace

Continued from page 34

almost all the way through one ball; remove skewer and press it through other side to make a bead. Leave bead on the skewer. In same fashion, "string" remaining beads on skewer. Suspend skewer between two books or other props so that beads do not touch any surface. Let beads air-dry.

2 Leaving hardened beads on skewer, use your fingertip to lightly coat beads with blue and purple powdered pigments. Spray beads with acrylic sealer; let dry.

3 Cut yarn into eight 6-inch pieces. From 22-gauge silver craft wire, cut eight 12-inch pieces. Wrap one end of a piece of wire three times around 4mm mandrel. Hold a piece of fuzzy yarn against wire and wrap it around mandrel. When no yarn

remains, wrap wire three times around mandrel and push the coil together so that it is 3/4–1 inch long. Then wrap wire diagonally back across coiled yarn. Use chain-nose pliers to press wire end into the yarn. Place a tiny drop of glue on any exposed yarn ends to prevent unraveling and fraying. Remove wire-yarn bead from mandrel. Repeat to make a total of eight wire-yarn beads.

4 String a crimp bead 1/2 inch from one end of beading wire; bend end through half of the clasp and back into crimp bead to form a loop. Crimp the crimp bead and string on one blue glass bead.

5 String on beads in the following order: yarn-wire, dotted spacer,

Create Use fuzzy yarn in a color that matches your favorite outfit; use different colors of pearlescent powdered pigments to give the beads a dressier look; add Swarovski crystal beads and shiny craft wire for a more elegant look.

light pink, dotted spacer, yarn-wire, dotted spacer, dark pink, blue glass, braided spacer, clay, braided spacer, blue glass, dark pink, dotted spacer.

6 Repeat beading pattern in step 5 until all yarn-wire beads are strung. Add a final blue glass bead, a crimp bead and remaining half of clasp. Bend end of flexible beading wire back into crimp bead to form loop and crimp the crimp bead. ◆

Candle Pedestal

It's hard to believe that this candle pedestal is created from a paper-clay base. Gold-highlighted paint creates a stonelike appearance.

Design by Koren Russell

The fibers brought to mind exotic places where candleholders would be forged by hand and beautified with fibers spun from silk.
—**Koren Russell**

Materials
- Paper-based air-drying clay
- Plastic foam: 2 (4 x 1-inch) discs, 3-inch ball, 3½-inch ball
- Antique bronze powdered pigment
- Black acrylic craft paint
- Paintbrush
- Fibers in 3 assorted, complementary styles
- 12 (8mm) bronze beads
- 5 inches 18-gauge copper wire
- Matte-finish varnish
- Tacky craft glue
- Pliers
- Serrated knife

Instructions

1 Using serrated knife, cut ¼ inch off top and bottom of both plastic foam balls. Cut 3½-inch ball in half; leave 3-inch ball in one piece.

2 Referring to photo throughout, glue wide end of each half-ball in center of a plastic foam disc. Glue other end of each half-ball to flattened end on 3-inch ball. Make sure pedestal is level and straight. Set aside to dry for 24 hours.

3 Pinch off bits of paper-based clay and press onto surface of plastic foam, pressing it into and across foam. Repeat to cover plastic foam pedestal with a thin, even, smooth layer of clay. Set aside to dry for 24 hours.

4 Paint pedestal black.

5 Mix powdered pigment with varnish to the consistency of paint. Dry-brush mixture lightly over the pedestal and set aside to dry.

6 Bend wire to form an L 1 inch from the end. Bend, twist and loop remaining wire, leaving 1-inch end straight. Push ½ inch of straight wire end into pedestal below top rim.

7 Cut a 32-inch strand of one fiber; knot ends together. Loop in half to form a doubled "necklace" and slip it over the straight wire, between the wire loops and the pedestal.

8 Repeat step 7 with second fiber.

9 Cut a 17-inch piece of the third fiber. String six beads onto fiber, knotting fiber before and after each bead to hold beads 2 inches apart. Knot ends of fiber together and slip loop over straight wire.

10 Repeat step 9 to create a second beaded fiber.

11 Push wire flush against pedestal. ◆

Treasure Bottles

Teeny, tiny glass beads embellish clear glass bottles that
will hold loose change, pretty stones or just wishes.

Design by Sandy L. Rollinger

Materials

- Glass spice jar
- Jute or metallic cord
- Jewel glue
- Microbeads
- Assorted larger beads
- Paper-based air-drying clay
- Chinese-character rubber stamp
- Powdered pigment
- Colored craft wire
- Craft varnish
- Glass cleaner
- Craft brush

I wanted to create a kind of genie-in-a-bottle look. I love fairy tales—yes, even now!—and these bottles remind me of something you would find in a treasure chest in a cave on a deserted island. After adding cord and paper-based clay embellishments, I thought they caught the look of lost treasure. I can envision them filled with expensive spices or even gold dust!

—Sandy L. Rollinger

Instructions

1 Clean jar with glass cleaner to remove any residue; let dry.

2 Drizzle white jewel glue randomly over one side of jar. Pour microbeads over glued areas and let dry undisturbed for at least one hour. Tap to remove excess beads. Repeat to glue beads to remaining sides of jar, letting glue dry after each application.

3 Apply craft varnish over beads; let dry.

4 Roll a small piece of paper-based clay into a thin, flat medallion about the size of a half-dollar. Tear little pieces from the edges.

5 Dip finger into powdered pigment and gently rub color onto clay. Stamp clay with rubber stamp and set medallion aside to dry.

6 String two or three larger beads onto each of three strands of selected fiber. Tie fibers around the neck of the bottle with beads dangling from ends.

7 Roll craft wire into a flat spiral; glue in upper left corner on one side of jar. Glue medallion over wire. Let glue dry thoroughly before using. ◆

Create Substitute leftover seed beads for the microbeads. Blend coordinating colors, add some bugle beads for extra sparkle, and apply to the jars according to the project instructions. Your bottles will take on a whole new look!

Floating Leaves Lamp Shade

Lightweight leaves of paper-based air-drying clay flutter softly on the sides of this lamp shade, while decorative glass beads add a fringy touch of drama!

Design by Vicki Schreiner

Instructions

1 Using ruler and pencil, lightly mark every ¾ inch around bottom of shade, just above edging. Punch a hole at each mark with hole punch.

Materials
- 7-inch lamp shade with 9-inch diameter across the bottom and 4-inch diameter across the top
- ⅛-inch tan eyelets
- Eyelet setting tool
- 3 complementary fibers
- Assorted glass beads in complementary shades, including E beads
- Clear nylon line
- Gunmetal 20-gauge craft wire
- Powdered pigments: spring green, sparkle copper
- Aspen leaf rubber stamp
- Clear adhesive
- Clear varnish
- ⅛-inch round hole punch
- Hammer
- Craft mat
- Wire cutters
- Rolling pin
- Paintbrush
- Baby powder
- Embroidery needle

2 *Set an eyelet into each hole:* Place eyelet in hole with shank inside shade. Lay shade on craft mat and position setter on shank. Hit setter with hammer to spread and flatten shank. Remove setter; carefully hit shank once or twice more to flatten it as much as possible.

3 *Working on one side of shade at a time, apply desired fibers around top and bottom:* Beginning at one corner of shade, place small bead of adhesive across shade as desired. Press one type fiber into adhesive. Continue around shade to form three or four tight rows. Add second type of fiber as desired over previous rows. Using an embroidery needle threaded with embroidery floss or another finer fiber, loosely weave a row of floss through previous rows as desired, hiding all knots under other fibers. Let dry.

4 Measure shade around bottom edge and cut a length of wire equal to at least three times this

measurement. Beginning at one corner of shade, thread wire through first eyelet from inside to outside of shade; pull wire through, leaving a 2-inch tail inside shade. Thread wire through next eyelet from inside to outside (wrapping wire over edge of shade) and pull snug without pulling it too tight. Continue in this manner all around shade. When finished, twist ends together inside shade; trim with wire cutters.

5 *Referring to beading diagram and photo throughout, assemble each strand of beaded fringe:* Cut 10-inch piece nylon line. Thread E bead onto strand and slide to center (Fig. 1). Fold nylon line in

Fig. 1   Fig. 2

> *This project was my chance to color outside the lines! I love the new nubby yarns, but have no time to crochet. I'm also caught up in the beading frenzy, and I've always wanted to try my hand at paper-based clay. Playing with these products to make this project was total enjoyment!*
>
> **—Vicki Schreiner**

half; holding ends even, thread both through each of the next three beads (Fig. 2). Knot ends of nylon line at bottom of a wire loop on shade (Fig. 3), then thread ends of nylon line back through beads and trim off excess line (Fig. 4).

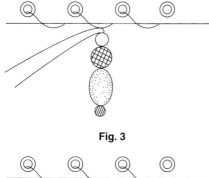

Fig. 3

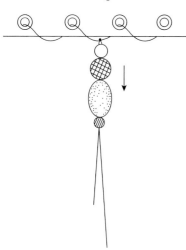

Fig. 4

6 *Leaves:* Knead half a package of paper-based clay until pliable. Slowly knead in small amounts of spring green powdered pigment until clay is light green (remember that color will lighten as clay dries).

7 Place paper towel on craft mat. Roll out light green clay ⅛ inch thick. Using rubber stamp, stamp desired number of leaves on clay (12 were used on sample). *Tip: Apply a small amount of baby powder to rolling pin and rubber stamp to prevent sticking.* Cut out each leaf with a craft knife using quick up-and-down motions. If desired, bend up the tips of some leaves to give them a nice dimensional look. Set leaves

on paper towel to air-dry completely (24–48 hours).

8 Use fingertip to apply sparkle copper pigment to front of each leaf and additional spring green pigment to edges and sides.

9 Apply two coats varnish to all surfaces of leaves, letting it dry between coats. When dry, glue leaves to lamp shade. ◆

Create
Give this design a whimsical look by making the leaves in bright colors and adding any of the sparkly fibers that are easily found in scrapbooking sections of craft shops. Large, boldly colored clear glass beads will refract the light and add to the magic of this project.

Wire-Adorned Mirror

Transform a yard-sale treasure into a fanciful wall accent with the addition of molded paper-clay accents and shiny beads.

Design by Lisa Galvin

Materials

- 8-inch-square frame with 3¾-inch mirror
- Dragonfly paper-casting mold
- Ready-to-use white paper-based air-drying clay
- Talc *or* cornstarch
- Rolling pin
- Baker's cooling rack
- Assorted coordinating fibers including metallic embroidery floss, decorative yarns, cords *and* feathers
- Khaki tan acrylic craft paint
- Paintbrushes: 1-inch glazing brush, #2 shader
- Water-based satin-finish varnish
- Straight-edge razor
- Powdered pigments: sunset gold, Aztec gold, sparkle copper
- 20-gauge gold wire
- Hot-glue gun
- Round-nose jewelry pliers
- Gem glue
- Window cleaner
- Paper towel *or* soft, lint-free cloth
- Picture hanger

Project Notes

Finished piece can be hung on a wall; or, for a glowing summer arrangement, lay frame flat on table and add a floating candle votive or small flower arrangement at center.

Instructions

1 Mix paper-based clay as directed by manufacturer; shape four 1½-inch balls. Use paintbrush to dust inside of casting mold with talc or cornstarch; turn mold over and tap bottom to remove excess. Place one clay ball in center of mold and roll with rolling pin to cover entire design. Remove from mold; cut desired border with scissors. (Do not let clay dry in the mold.) Repeat with remaining clay to create a total of four dragonflies.

2 Give a "marbled" effect to the next layer of clay by mixing in assorted fibers. Cut ¼- to ¾-inch pieces of floss, cord, yarn and feathers. Form a fist-size lump of clay into a bowl-like shape and sprinkle fibers in bowl. Fold in sides of bowl and knead. If you have trouble distributing the fibers evenly throughout the clay, begin pulling to "tear" the clay, then put back together and knead again. Repeat until fibers are thoroughly mixed in.

3 Using a rolling pin, roll clay into a flat sheet ⅛ inch thick and at least 3 inches wide. One at a time, moisten back of dragonfly pieces with water and place on clay/fiber sheet, positioning them to leave a border of at least ½ inch of fiber/clay around each shape. The water will effectively glue the dragonfly shapes to the fiber/clay backing. Cut around shapes with scissors, leaving ⅜-inch border; set dragonflies on cooling rack to dry.

4 Using glaze brush, paint frame with two or three coats of khaki tan; let dry. Brush frame with varnish; let dry.

5 Dip shader brush first into varnish and then into sunset gold powdered pigment and lightly brush along edges and randomly on top of frame to accent, reloading brush as necessary. Let dry. Attach hanger to back.

6 Working with one dragonfly at a time, brush body with varnish, then dip brush into sunset gold powdered pigment and return brush to wet varnish. In same fashion, add Aztec gold coloring to dragonfly wings. For added highlight, brush sparkle copper along outer edges of wings where they join body; let dry.

7 For an "aged" appearance, randomly brush outer edges and top of clay with varnish and sunset gold powdered pigment.

8 Hot-glue clay squares to corners of frame.

9 Cut random lengths of gold wire, then curl one end with round-nose pliers. Slip beads onto wires, then bend wires to create swirled "flight paths" for dragonflies. Insert each straight end of wire between clay layers near dragonfly "tail" to create small hole. Remove wire, apply a drop of gem glue to end and reinsert into hole. Arrange beads, holding them in fixed position with small drops of gem glue applied to wire.

10 Clean stray brush marks and excess paint from front of mirror using straight-edge razor. Clean mirror with window cleaner and paper towel. ◆

Create

Molds come in all different shapes and sizes. Give this mirror a masculine look by substituting leaf motifs and using deeper colors of beads and wire to make a great wall accent for a den or office.

Perhaps better titled "Dance of the Dragonflies," this project combines some of my favorite "ingredients" and was fun to create! With its beaded-wire flight path, these paper-mold-cast dragonflies dusted with metallic pigments seem to spring to life—adding an attractive dimensional effect to an otherwise basic wooden frame.

—Lisa Galvin

FEATHERS
Acrylic Paint
Paper
Mosaic Tiles
PLASTIC FOAM

Plastic foam is a sturdy, lightweight material that can be the base of a project or just an accent. Combined with other craft supplies, it becomes a fashionable home accent!

Nautical Adventures Frame

The challenge—each designer needs to create a project using the materials we selected (and one or two more items they add).

Design by June Fiechter

Materials

- DecoArt decorating paste
- Walnut Hollow 13 x 11-inch wooden frame with oval opening #23254
- Styrofoam brand plastic foam pieces from Dow: large sheet, small egg, large hen egg, 4-inch cone, 1-inch ball
- Sharp serrated knife
- Tacky craft glue
- Earthtone ⅜-inch mosaic tiles #MS253 from Jennifer's Mosaics
- Pheasant feathers from Zucker Feather Products
- Acrylic craft paints: green, deep burgundy, gray-blue, light cinnamon brown
- 6 clear glass pebbles from Jennifer's Mosaics
- Glaze/wash paintbrush
- Gold mulberry paper from Stampin' Up
- Rub-on transfer with desired saying
- Heavenly gold #DHH17 Hevenly Hues Plaster & Ceramic Wash from DecoArt
- Hold the Foam glue from Beacon Adhesives

"*I really enjoy working with the foam and opted to create a picture rather than a frame. My daughter thought of the sailboat theme, and I found that the foam pieces were perfect for making boats. Glass pebbles are usually a favorite of mine for crafting, but I didn't want them to take away from the scene I created, so I incorporated only a few clear ones.*"

—June Fiechter

Instructions

1 Cut large foam sheet to fit front of frame; cut 5½ x 3½-inch oval in upper left corner to correspond with opening in frame; glue Styrofoam in place on front of frame. Cut another piece to fit in frame opening; glue in place. Cut a 4⅛ x 2½-inch oval; set aside for now.

2 Cut large hen egg in half; set aside one piece for another use and cut second half in half again. Referring to photo throughout, use plastic foam glue to glue these pieces in place at bottom of frame for boats.

3 Using photo for guide, cut waves from flat sheet of

Continued on page 53

Craft Closet Challenge

My Eccentric Garden

Design by Judi Kauffman

Materials

- DecoArt decorating paste
- Palette knife or craft stick
- Walnut Hollow 13 x 11-inch wooden frame with oval opening #23254
- Styrofoam brand plastic foam pieces from Dow: half of a 2½-inch ball; half of a 1-inch ball; 3 halves cut lengthwise from 1½-inch eggs
- Hold the Foam glue from Beacon Adhesives
- Kids Choice Fast-Grab Glue from Beacon Adhesives
- Toothpick or corsage pin
- Small, sharp, pointed scissors
- Assorted square mosaic tiles and round, flat marbles
- Acrylic craft paints: black, deep iridescent gold
- Paintbrush
- Stencil brush
- Stampin' Up mulberry papers: yellow, tan, brown, green, rust
- Matte-finish acrylic adhesive medium
- Almond feathers (#PH Plumage Almond LSE Nat #B552) from Zucker Feather Products
- Corrugated cardboard
- Complementary velvet fabric
- Batting

Instructions

1. Referring to photo throughout, use pencil to sketch stems, flowers and leaves on frame. Glue Styrofoam pieces in place for flower centers with plastic foam glue.

Continued on page 68

I had never considered feathers, paper, plastic foam and mosaics as components for the same project. To unify everything, I decided to think of the mosaics as textural elements, ignoring the colors, covering them with torn paper and then painting them to coordinate with the feathers. I wanted to create something that looked old, but also elegant. I chose to use the feathers as petals and brought attention to the otherwise plain oval flower by padding velvet and adding vintage pins, turning it into the focal point of the project.

—Judi Kauffman

Craft Closet Challenge
Glamour Girl Lipstick Mirror

Design by Mary Lynn Maloney

Materials

- DecoArt decorating paste
- Walnut Hollow 13 x 11-inch wooden frame with oval opening #23254
- Acrylic craft paints: flesh tone, vanilla, winter blue
- Bronze metallic acrylic paint
- Polyform Shapelets stylized lotus template
- Vintage glamour girl and cosmetic ads from Dover Publications' *Advertising Art in the Art Deco Style*
- Stampin' Up mulberry papers: 2 sheets each yellow and olive green
- Pheasant feathers from Zucker Feather Products: 8 (1½- to 2-inch), 1 (4-inch)
- Dark blue ½-inch round glass pebbles from Diamond Tech International
- 3 Styrofoam brand plastic foam 1-inch balls from Dow
- ⅜-inch-square mosaic tiles from Jennifer's Mosaics from Diamond Tech International: ivory, terra-cotta
- Piece of scrap paper
- Paintbrush
- Wooden craft sticks
- White craft glue
- Gem glue
- Hold the Foam glue from Beacon Adhesives
- 4 x 6-inch mirror

I kept looking at this frame vertically rather than horizontally. Then it struck me that the little oval opening would make an ideal lipstick mirror. I envisioned how this might look in a 1920s lady's powder room and my project is the result.

—Mary Lynn Maloney

Instructions

1 Apply a light, random coat of flesh tone paint to entire wooden frame. Follow with a light random coat of vanilla; let dry.

2 Crumple a piece of scrap paper into a ball; dampen with water. Referring to photo throughout, use paper ball to "sponge" winter blue randomly over surface of frame, twisting ball as you go and creating brush strokes. Let dry.

3 Place lotus template at one corner of frame. Using craft stick, spread a thin layer of decorating paste over template opening. Lift template straight up off surface. Wash template with water; dry. Repeat process in remaining corners; let dry.

4 Lightly brush bronze paint over stenciled shapes, paying special attention to edges.

5 Cut four or five selected images from book of advertising images. Tear the edges of some of the images for added textural interest. Tear mulberry paper into pieces of various sizes. Mix one part craft glue with two parts water. Arrange images and paper pieces in a pleasing arrangement on frame. Use glue mixture to decoupage papers and images onto frame. Overlap bits of paper with some images. Brush a final coat of glue-water mixture over all; let dry.

6 Apply a drop of craft glue at pointed end of one bronzed lotus shape; press ends of two feathers into glue and arrange so that feathers follow shape of lotus. Repeat on remaining lotus shapes.

7 Using gem glue, attach a dark blue glass pebble over feathers at each corner.

8 Cut Styrofoam balls in half. Using glue-water mixture, glue bits of both mulberry papers over each ball half. Let dry.

9 Brush a small amount of bronze paint over each ball to highlight raised areas. Using plastic foam glue, glue a Styrofoam half-ball in each corner as shown. Glue remaining half-balls directly under upper two blue pebbles.

10 Mix one part bronze paint with two parts decorating paste. Using craft stick, spread a narrow line of mixture along one edge of frame. Press ivory and terra-cotta mosaic tiles into paste, alternating colors, and adding two dark blue glass pebbles as you go. Repeat on remaining edges of frame.

11 Glue 4-inch feather directly on collage. Insert mirror in oval opening. ◆

Nautical Adventures Frame
Continued from page 50

Styrofoam; glue at bottom of frame under boats.

4 Cut Styrofoam cone in half; glue pieces in place above boats for sails.

5 Cut Styrofoam ball in half; glue pieces above sails.

6 Cut Styrofoam small egg in half; press pieces into shape of flags and glue below balls.

7 Spread decorating paste over all Styrofoam pieces. While paste is still wet, press glass pebbles into all corners and on top of balls; press

brown square tiles along top edge of boats; cut fluffy fibers from spine of feathers and let them fall into the wet paste. Let dry.

8 Cut stars from gold paper; glue randomly over sky area.

9 Blend gray-blue paint with water to create a wash; paint background with mixture, keeping paint away from the paper stars, which would soak up the color.

10 In the same fashion, make paint-water washes with deep burgundy, cinnamon brown and green paints. Paint boats and flags with deep burgundy wash, cinnamon brown wash for sails and green for water, letting wash dry between applications.

11 Following manufacturer's instructions, rub transfer onto Styrofoam oval cut in step 1.

12 Rub all pieces with metallic gold wash, again avoiding the paper stars.

13 Glue a few scraps of Styrofoam onto back of oval for spacers, then glue oval in oval opening in upper left corner. ◆

Fisherman's Theme Creel

Broken glass pieces are put back together
to create a unique fish motif.

Design by Lisa Galvin

Materials
- 11 x 11 x 7-inch creel basket
- Acrylic craft paints: raw sienna, burnt umber, red, white
- Palette
- Matte-finish spray acrylic sealer
- Pieces or chips of stained glass: green, red, white
- ¼-inch brass foil tape
- Clear glass gems
- 24-gauge plastic-coated wire: icy copper, clear silver
- Small white glass heart-shaped bead
- ⅝-inch finished wooden bead with ⅛-inch opening
- 1½-inch Styrofoam brand plastic foam ball
- 4½-inch piece wooden skewer or ¹¹⁄₆₄-inch dowel
- Feathered spinner-style fishing lure
- 15-inch piece ⅛-inch latigo-style leather lace
- 2 or 3 decorative feathers
- ½-inch letter rubber stamps
- Pigment or embossing stamp ink pad
- Cream-colored moiré paper
- Copper embossing powder
- Heat gun
- Dried and/or silk floral leaf stems
- Decorative moss
- Drill with ⁹⁄₆₄-inch bit
- Fine sandpaper
- Hammer or glass pliers
- Safety goggles
- Pliers
- Cone-shaped coffee filters
- Paper grocery sack
- Strainer
- Craft knife
- Hot-glue gun
- Transparent-drying glue sticks
- Craft stick
- 1½-inch flat bristle paintbrush
- Cutting mat

Creel

1 *Painting:* Dilute some raw sienna paint with a little water on palette. Dry-brush basket inside and out with mixture (refer to directions for dry-brushing under "Painting Techniques" in the General Instructions, page 174). Blend a small amount of burnt umber onto palette and repeat dry-brushing until desired weathered effect is achieved, darkening some areas more than others, and paying special attention to those areas that might take more abuse over time—front, edges of lid, etc. Let dry.

2 Sand edges of creel lightly, again taking into consideration which edges might be subjected to more wear and tear. Wipe off dust, then spray creel with acrylic sealer; let dry.

This basket was not only fun and easy to create, it took me down memory lane to my childhood years when I would go fishing in the lakes of Minnesota with my grandfather—always in the wee hours of the morning.

—Lisa Galvin

3 *Basket closure:* Drill two holes at bottom edge of basket lid. Slip ends of a 6-inch piece of lace through holes from front to back and knot ends to hold in place. Thread wooden bead onto remaining lace; knot one end and slide bead to knot. Thread unknotted end through weave in creel below lid loop and knot inside, checking fit of ball in loop; trim off excess leather lace.

Stained Glass Fish

1 *Preparing glass:* This project— especially the bobber—takes relatively small pieces of glass, so you will need to break or cut pieces into the sizes needed. Wear safety goggles. If glass pliers are not available, place glass chips into cone-shaped coffee filter. Place filter in paper sack and lay on hard surface, then tap lightly with hammer. (If you are starting with larger pieces of glass, place them first in a paper grocery sack and tap with hammer to make smaller pieces that are easier to handle before placing them in the coffee filter.) Place filter upright in strainer and rinse under running water to separate small particles and dust from pieces you'll be using. Remove unwanted points or sharp edges with pliers; place glass pieces on paper towel to dry. Repeat with all colors of glass.

2 *Planning glass placement:* Referring to photo throughout, arrange glass pieces to determine placement. **Note:** *Reassembly will be much easier if you trace the shapes in order of assembly on a piece of scrap paper.* First arrange green glass chips to create fish.

3 Wrap edges of glass pieces with foil tape, overlapping ends slightly and smoothing excess over edges on both sides with a craft stick held flat.

4 Prop creel lid so that it lies flat. Use gem glue to glue glass pieces to lid and glue bead in place for eye.

Bobber

1 Paint bottom half (pointed end) of skewer white and top half red; let dry. Insert painted skewer through center of Styrofoam ball.

2 Hot-glue small red and white glass pieces to ball (matching to paint color), leaving about a quarter of ball's surface uncoated on back to attach to basket.

3 Wrap copper wire five or six times around skewer near top of bobber; form loop. Slip silver wire through loop; twist, then cut, leaving 10–12 inches of wire. Hot-glue bobber and moss to creel as shown and arrange silver wire so that bobber appears to be tangled in the "branches."

Lure

1 Using wire cutters, clip sharp hooks off lure; discard hooks. For decorative hook, cut two 5-inch pieces copper wire; fold in half and twist together, leaving a loop at top to attach to lure and 1 inch of each exposed end remaining. Cut one wire end and discard. Curl loop at ends of remaining three wires and bend to create hook shapes, replicating a three-pronged hook. Attach hook to lure with a small piece of wire, twisting to hold in place.

2 Place decorative feathers behind lure and wrap at top with copper wire; slip wire ends through weave in basket and twist to hold lure in place. To give lure the appearance of dangling from the basket, slip silver wire through eye hook at top of lure, twist wire together, bring remaining length to inside of basket, through basket weave. Clip and trim ends.

"Bubbles"

1 Stamp "GO FISH" on moiré paper; apply embossing powder and heat to emboss.

2 Hot-glue flat surface of a clear glass gem over each letter. Place on cutting mat; using craft knife, cut paper closely around bottoms of gems. Hot-glue letters to lid so that they appear to be bubbles coming from fish's mouth.

3 Hot-glue remaining floral accents and gems to lid. ◆

Colors of Nature Collage

Geometric foam shapes embellished with handmade paper and feathers create "reach out and touch" texture.

Design by Mary Lynn Maloney

Materials

- 14 x 18-inch stretched canvas
- Iridescent acrylic paints: pearl blue, russet, bronze, pink-gold, blue-gold
- 6-inch squares of origami mesh paper: yellow, red, purple, blue, orange
- Assorted lightweight mulberry and fibrous papers: purple, off-white, sage green, lime green
- 5 natural skeleton leaves
- Styrofoam brand plastic foam pieces: 11⅞ x ¹⁵⁄₁₆-inch-thick disc; 9-inch x 3⅞-inch cone; 1-inch ball
- Pheasant feathers
- Teal stained glass tiles
- 3 (12- to 15-inch) twigs
- Styrofoam cutter or serrated knife
- Styrofoam glue
- Gem glue
- Clear-drying white craft glue

Project Note

The shorter sides of the stretched canvas are the top and bottom edges.

Instructions

1 Referring to photo throughout, apply random strokes of all colors of iridescent paints over canvas, overlapping some colors to create depth. Paint edges of canvas solid blue; let dry.

2 Mix one part white craft glue with two parts water. Arrange origami mesh squares down center of canvas, overlapping colors. Add a narrow strip of mesh to upper left portion of canvas and two narrow strips horizontally along lower third of canvas. Brush glue-water mixture over mesh to adhere pieces to canvas; let dry.

3 Cut Styrofoam disc in half into half-moon shape; reserve one piece for another use. Cut cone into quarters; set aside two for another use. Trim tips from remaining two so that they measure 6 inches in length. Using glue-water mixture, adhere torn pieces of purple and sage green papers to half-moon and quarter-cones. Cut Styrofoam ball in half; set aside one piece for another use. Cover remaining half with lime and sage green paper pieces. Let dry.

4 Brush undiluted white glue along straight edge of half-moon; adhere pheasant feathers along edge. In same fashion, adhere pheasant feathers along bottom edge of canvas. Let dry.

5 Glue one skeleton leaf in center of half-moon; glue two or three feathers at base of leaf.

6 Use Styrofoam glue to glue half-moon to upper right area of canvas; glue cone shapes to bottom left and right edges as shown, one pointing up and one pointing down.

7 Glue remaining skeleton leaves as shown, one horizontally on narrow strip of mesh, and three vertically over narrow mesh near bottom of canvas. Let dry.

8 Position twigs as shown; glue in place. Glue Styrofoam half-ball to upper point of half-moon. Let dry.

9 Mix one part iridescent blue paint with two parts gem glue. Using mixture, glue assorted stained glass tiles to collage as shown, along left edge of narrow mesh strip, and along inner edges of quarter-cones. Allow glue-paint mixture to ooze out from tiles, adding color and acting as grout. Let dry. ◆

Create

Go a little crazy in combining unique materials to create your own nature collage. Feel free to add pebbles, leaves, pinecones and other natural elements.

Autumn is my favorite season, partly because of all the rich colors I associate with it. The temperature where I live started climbing toward 100 when I started this collage. The beginning of a long, hot summer always makes me wish for fall.

—Mary Lynn Maloney

Fractured Sunflower Altered Book

Handmade paper and broken china pieces create a stylized sunflower accent.

Design by Chris Malone

Instructions

1 Open book to midpoint; apply craft glue generously to edges of pages on top, bottom and sides; let dry.

Materials

- Old book (sample measures 8½ x 5½ inches)
- Styrofoam brand plastic foam pieces: 3³⁄₁₆- x 2⅞-inch egg, 1-inch ball
- Foam picnic plate
- Ceramic plate with colorful design (plate used for sample had yellow roses)
- 4 red glass pebbles
- Assorted textured papers
- Assorted feathers
- Assorted fibers: yarn, thin ribbon, metallic cord
- Acrylic paints in complementary colors (dark red, tan, gold and three shades of green were used on sample)
- Foam finish
- Spray matte finish
- Craft glue
- Jewel glue
- Paintbrushes: flat, liner
- Sea sponge
- Craft knife
- Toothpicks
- Hammer
- Old towels
- Large-eye needle

2 If desired, paint edges of pages to coordinate with cover. Sample was painted dark red at top and bottom with a red wash on side edges.

3 Dip a damp sea sponge into tan background color; pat unevenly over both pages and side edges of book; let dry.

4 Tear rectangles from paper. Glue pieces, overlapping, to each page. On sample, leaf page has a long cream rectangle and small gold rectangle; flower page has cream, red and patterned tan covering most of page.

5 Cut four lengthwise slices from Styrofoam egg, each at least 2½ inches long and ³⁄₁₆–¼ inch deep. Using leaf pattern and craft knife, cut leaf from each piece.

6 For tassel top, push toothpick all the way through Styrofoam ball; enlarge one hole a little.

7 Following manufacturer's instructions, coat all Styrofoam pieces with foam finish; let dry. *Note: Insert two toothpicks into flat bottom of each leaf for coating and drying.*

8 Paint tassel top; on sample, it is painted dark red to coordinate with book and feathers. Paint leaves green; using sponge, highlight edges with a lighter shade of green.

9 From foam picnic plate cut two pieces 2 x 3 inches. Using toothpick or pen, trace around leaf pattern onto each piece, pressing hard enough to make an indented line but not so hard as to cut through plate. Apply green paint to leaf only; press to page and carefully lift straight up. Using same "stamp," repeat to make second leaf. In same fashion, use second leaf stamp to stamp two gold leaves. Let dry.

10 Glue Styrofoam leaves to plate, between and overlapping stamped leaves. Thin dark green paint; using liner, draw vein lines on stamped and painted leaves.

11 Tear a small piece of gold paper into a leaf shape; glue to composition. Spray pages with matte finish; let dry.

12 Using jewel glue, attach three glass pebbles to page for berries.

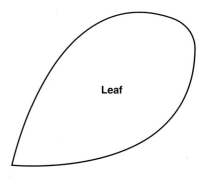

Leaf

For me, nature is the most inspiring and versatile subject for a collage or altered book. Almost any kind of craft product can be manipulated into something that fits the theme! The curved feathers made me think of a fluffy tassel to finish off this project.

—Chris Malone

13 Wrap plate in towels; hit with hammer to break into small pieces. Glue remaining glass pebble to page and arrange colored shards from plate around pebble in flower shape, adding green pieces at edge for leaves.

When satisfied with placement, secure with jewel glue.

14 Thread large-eye needle with two 8-inch fibers. Insert needle into large hole of ball, up through top and back again, leaving a small loop at top. Hold loop by slipping a pencil through it while finishing tassel. Cut smooth ends off three or four feathers so that fluffy ends remain. Dip each tip in glue, then push up into large hole. Wrap assorted fibers around binding of book and tie in knot near bottom inside of book. Clip ends to about 3 inches. Slip one strong fiber through loop of

Create

Experiment with other colors and shapes of china to create different flower motifs.

tassel top and tie in knot to secure.

15 Glue two feather ends (cut from tassel feathers) to flower page if desired. ◆

Blazing Sun Garden Thermometer

Painted gold tiles create a glowing sun with Southwest flair.

Design by Lorine Mason

Materials

- Thermometer with plastic base
- Terra-cotta tiles *or* broken flowerpots
- 9 x 15 x 1-inch sheet Styrofoam brand plastic foam
- Balsa wood: 3 x 10-inch piece, ¼-inch-thick, for base; 1¼ x 45-inch strip, ⅛-inch-thick, for sides
- Paper napkin with leaf and acorn design
- 10 x 16-inch piece thin cardboard
- Nonsanded grout
- Antique gold acrylic craft paint
- Feathers
- 1-inch-wide elastic
- Tile nippers *or* pliers
- Thick craft glue
- Decoupage medium
- Satin-finish varnish
- Screwdriver
- Sponge
- Paintbrush
- Serrated knife
- Craft knife
- Miter box
- Sawtooth picture hanger
- Safety goggles

Instructions

1 Cut Styrofoam to a point at one end by measuring up 3½ inches from each side; mark, then place a mark at center point. Draw a diagonal line from center mark to each side mark; cut point using serrated knife.

2 Separate top printed layer from napkin; tear it into 2- and 3-inch pieces.

3 Cover front surfaces of balsa base and strip for sides with decoupage medium. Lay torn pieces of napkin into medium, overlapping edges and adding additional decoupage medium over top of all pieces. Let dry.

4 Remove thermometer from plastic base; attach to 3 x 10-inch balsa base. Center on plastic foam and glue in place.

5 Put on safety goggles. Using nippers or pliers, break terra-cotta tile or flowerpots into many pieces no larger than 1½ inches. Start by choosing pieces suitable for the sun's rays; set sun in upper left corner, securing pieces with thick craft glue. Continue adding pieces until entire surface is covered, trimming pieces as needed with tile nippers. Let dry overnight.

6 Measure and cut 1¼-inch balsa strips to fit around all sides of plastic foam base; use miter box when cutting corners.

7 Apply a generous amount of glue to backs of all balsa pieces; glue to sides of Styrofoam. Wrap circumference of piece with elastic and tie tightly. Wrap additional elastic tightly around front and back in at least two places; let dry.

8 Remove elastic. Following manufacturer's instructions, apply grout. Let dry, then wipe residue off tiles with dampened sponge.

9 Decoupage mitered corners and touch up any damaged areas with additional pieces of napkin. Let dry.

10 Using gold paint, paint tiles used for sun and top edge of wooden frame. Let dry.

11 Spray entire surface with two or three coats varnish, letting it dry between coats.

12 Glue a cluster of feathers to bottom of thermometer. Glue a piece of tile on top of feather ends. Weight down tile with a heavy object; let dry.

13 Apply generous layer of glue to back of completed thermometer and place on top of cardboard. Weight down with heavy object and let dry. Trim edges of cardboard with craft knife. Attach hanger, applying glue to ends of nails. ◆

Once the design is chosen, mosaics are just plain puzzle-style fun. Finding the first perfect piece is almost as satisfying as fitting in the last piece. The design is always a pleasant surprise to me once the last bit of grout is wiped off the finished project.
—Lorine Mason

Serene Reflections Set

Broken mirrors don't have to mean bad luck!
Use the pieces to add a sparkling touch to a dresser set.

Designs by Sandy L. Rollinger

Materials

Each Project
- Gold acrylic paint
- Small mirror tiles
- Small pieces of white-and-gold handmade paper
- Matte-finish decoupage glue/sealer
- Brushes: 1-inch flat craft brush, smaller paintbrush
- Jewel glue
- Small plastic sandwich bag
- Towel
- Small hammer
- Disposable plate

Frame
- 5 x 7-inch plastic foam frame
- 4 narrow feathers, at least 6 inches long (see Project Note)
- Small piece of household sponge
- Double-sided tape
- Frame stand

Box
- 5-inch square wooden craft box with lid
- 1-inch Styrofoam brand plastic foam ball
- Sandpaper
- Peacock herl (small feathers from a shaft of peacock feather; see Project Note)

Project Note
Feathers are available at craft stores and fly-tying shops.

Frame

1. Pour a small amount of gold paint onto a disposable plate. Dip sponge into paint and apply to front and back of foam frame; let dry.

2. Using 1-inch brush, apply decoupage sealer down right side and across top of frame.

3. Referring to photo throughout, press three long feathers into sealer on frame as shown. Coat lightly with decoupage sealer; let dry.

4. Apply additional sealer to top right corner of frame. Cut a small triangle from a piece of paper and press into sealer on corner and over edges; coat with more sealer and let dry.

5. Form last feather in a figure 8; glue in top corner near paper.

6. Place mirror tiles in plastic bag. Place bag on a hard surface like a breadboard or cement floor. Cover bag with towel and use hammer to gently break tiles into fragments.

7. Carefully remove fragments from bag; using jewel glue, glue fragments in center of feather bow as shown. Let dry.

8. Affix photo behind opening in frame with strips of double-sided tape. Place finished frame in stand.

Box

1. Lightly sand box and lid; wipe off dust.

2. Pour a small amount of gold paint onto a disposable plate. Using 1-inch brush, paint box, lid and foam ball; let dry. Give box and lid a second coat of paint; let dry.

3. Using smaller brush, apply decoupage sealer to one side of box. Referring to photo throughout, press feathers into wet sealer in random fashion. Apply another coat of sealer over feathers. In this fashion, apply sealer and feathers to all sides of box and to top of lid.

4. Cut small triangles from paper; using sealer as in step 3, press triangles randomly over surface of box and lid. Apply another coat of decoupage sealer over all; let dry.

5. Slightly flatten ball on one side. Apply glue to flattened surface and press onto center of lid; let dry.

6. Place mirror tiles in plastic bag. Place bag on a hard surface like a bread board or cement floor. Cover bag with towel and use hammer to break tiles into fragments.

7. Carefully remove fragments from bag; arrange randomly on box and lid. When satisfied with arrangement, secure fragments with jewel glue; let dry. ◆

I was inspired to create this project because I wanted something functional as well as a decorative, artistic piece. The mosaics were made from fragmented mirror tiles. I wanted something more delicate for a small project, and the mirror tiles added just enough sparkle. I also wanted the feathers to complement the delicacy of the mirrors and that is why I chose smaller, finer feathers.
—**Sandy L. Rollinger**

Frosted Dragonflies Tray

Patterned paper makes finishing this tray a snap!

Design by Sherian Frey

Materials

- 12 x 16-inch rectangular wooden tray
- Decorative paper in 2 complementary patterns, one simpler and one more complex
- 4 x 6-inch white tissue paper
- Decoupage glue/sealer
- Square transparent acrylic mosaic tiles in colors to complement papers
- Acrylic paints in one light color and one dark color to match colors in tiles and papers
- Paintbrushes: 1-inch and ¼-inch flats
- 2 yards complementary craft cord
- 1-inch Styrofoam brand plastic foam ball
- Clear acrylic spray sealer
- 4–6 feathers
- Masking tape (optional)
- Craft glue
- Fine sandpaper

Instructions

1 Referring to photo throughout, paint bottom, sides and ⅛ inch around top edge of tray with darker paint. Add a ¼-inch band of lighter color around top and bottom of recessed area in middle of tray. Paint rise of recessed area with lighter color. If using tray without a recessed area, paint ½-inch band of lighter color 2 inches from side. Let dry. Sand lightly with fine sandpaper; wipe off dust.

2 Repeat step 1, omitting sanding step if desired.

3 Paint Styrofoam ball with lighter color. Let dry, then paint again.

4 Decoupage top of tray with decorative papers following instructions on jar of glue/sealer. Allow papers to cover edges of painted areas. Fit center/bottom paper to corners of recess.

5 Tear white tissue paper into irregular pieces no larger than ¼ inch by ¼ inch. Coat ball with decoupage sealer. While ball is still wet, use paintbrush to pick up and place tissue. Apply two or three layers of tissue to cover ball completely; paint color will be muted, but will still show slightly. Allow sealer to dry completely.

6 Glue mosaic pieces in place; let dry.

7 Glue cord in place, outlining mosaic pieces and covering edge of paper. Let dry.

Any of the elements can be changed to personalize this tray—try substituting broken pieces of mirror for the plastic tiles.

Create

8 Seal entire tray with clear acrylic spray following manufacturer's instructions.

9 Cut Styrofoam ball in half; seal with acrylic spray. Glue feathers and half-balls to tray as shown, planning the arrangement before you apply the glue, and applying glue to feathers only on the bottom tips that will be concealed by Styrofoam. **Note:** *Once glue is tacky enough to hold half-balls* in place, flip tray; tray's weight will press Styrofoam firmly in place until dry.

10 **Project Note:** *Clean tray with a damp cloth, but do not submerge tray in water.* ◆

I love the outdoors, subtle color variations and unity. This serving tray allows the combination of all three. The decoupage layering of papers allowed me to repeat the paper used on the outer portion of the tray by placing it under the more transparent paper of the dragonflies, providing both unity and subtle color. The decorative feathers repeat both the dots of the paper and the wings of the dragonfly. The Styrofoam brand balls also repeat the dots; the "color showing through" provided subtle color unity and added dimension to the project.

—Sherian Frey

Princess Memory Box

Pink feathers add a funky touch to the lid of this cache box.

Design by Samantha McNesby

Materials
- Acrylic craft paints: medium pink, white
- 1 sheet pink tissue paper
- 3 (2½-inch) Styrofoam brand plastic foam balls
- Serrated knife *or* plastic-foam knife
- Pink marabou feathers
- 8 (¾-inch) white glass mosaic tiles
- 10-inch-diameter round papier-mâché box with lid
- Medium- or chisel-tip silver paint pen
- Transfer paper
- Craft cement
- Thick white craft glue
- Paintbrushes: 1-inch foam brush, 1-inch scruffy brush

Make this fun and funky keepsake box for your favorite little princess. It is large enough to hold all sorts of special mementos and is a great alternative to a scrapbook or album.
—Samantha McNesby

Instructions

1 Using foam brush, paint box and lid white; let dry. Paint box and lid with two coats medium pink, letting paint dry between applications.

2 Thin a small amount of white paint with an equal amount of water. Working on one area at a time, use scruffy brush and a pouncing, up-and-down motion to dab mixture onto outside of box, then blot with a paper towel. Allow some of the base color to show through. Let dry.

3 Referring to photo throughout and to instructions for "Using Transfer & Graphite Paper" (General Instructions, page 174), use pencil and transfer paper to transfer "Princess" lettering onto lid. Paint lettering with silver paint pen.

4 Using silver pen, outline edges of box lid and base, and edges of each mosaic tile. Let dry.

5 Using serrated knife, cut ½-inch slice from each Styrofoam ball. Cover each ball with pink tissue paper using thick white glue; let dry.

6 Using thick white glue, glue feathers around rim of box lid; let dry.

7 Using glass cement, glue tiles to rim of lid on top of feathers, pressing tiles firmly against box lid and spacing them evenly. Let dry.

8 Turn box upside down on flat surface. Glue flat sides of tissue-covered balls to bottom of box for legs. Let box dry for 24 hours before using. ◆

Create Personalize the colors of this treasure box to suit your own little princess.

Princess

Princess

Lettering

My Eccentric Garden
Continued from page 51

2 Using palette knife or craft stick, apply decorating paste in a thick layer, one area at a time, and attach tiles and flat marbles; begin with flower centers and petals, then stems, then leaves, then border. On small flowers, add a second layer of tiles and marbles for dimension.

3 Swirl decorating paste on remaining surface for a textured background.

4 Tear mulberry paper into small pieces and form a collage over all of the decorating paste, one color at a time. Using a brush dipped in acrylic adhesive medium, press paper into crevices, covering all the decorating paste. Use tan for the background, rust for daisy and round flower petals, green for stems, leaves and bottom border, yellow for daisy center and small flowers, and brown for round flower center.

5 Dab stencil brush into black paint; wipe off most of the paint onto a paper towel. Using almost-dry brush, lightly brush all high points of mosaics, applying color darkest on daisy petals, stems and leaves. Make sure that paper colors remain visible in some areas.

6 Paint edges of wooden frame black.

7 Dab stencil brush into iridescent gold paint; wipe off most of the paint onto a paper towel. Using almost-dry brush, lightly highlight center of daisy, border, around oval and background. Let paints dry.

8 Glue feathers around large oval "flower"—the oval opening—in upper right corner of frame, positioning quill points between round marble shapes.

9 Cut cardboard to fit snugly in oval opening. Cover with batting, then velvet fabric, pulling edges neatly and smoothly to back; glue to secure. Glue covered oval in opening in frame; use as a showcase for a favorite vintage brooch or two. ◆

Travel Memories Album

A plastic foam frame makes a base in which
to embed beads and other interesting embellishments.

Design by Katie Hacker

Materials

- Blue 5¼ x 7-inch "brag book" photo album
- 5 x 7-inch Styrofoam brand picture frame
- Assorted 1- to 2-inch paper art images
- Assorted blue patterned papers
- 2 light blue 2- or 3-inch feathers
- 2 (¾-inch) square blue glass mosaic tiles
- 2 (½-inch) pieces sea glass
- 52 (½-inch) gold head pins
- 52 blue "E" beads
- Blue acrylic craft paint
- Heavy-duty sewing needle
- Acrylic sealer
- Collage gel
- Craft glue or hot glue
- Sponge paintbrush

Instructions

1 Paint inside rim of frame blue; let dry.

2 Tear 1- to 2-inch pieces from blue patterned paper. Using sponge brush, spread collage gel over back of each piece, then press onto frame, wrapping paper around outer edges and pressing out bubbles with your fingers. Carefully tear off any paper that extends over photo opening.

3 Referring to photo throughout, glue paper art images to frame as shown: two in upper left corner, one in

There is nothing like traveling to renew your spirit and fill you with a sense of adventure. My trips to Europe were the inspiration behind this memory album. I used faux postage stamps, postmarks and other travel-inspired ephemera to create a decorative collage.
—**Katie Hacker**

upper right corner, one at lower right edge of photo opening and two at lower left edge of photo opening. Seal frame with a very thin layer of sealer (too much will cause paper to bubble).

4 Use heavy-duty sewing needle to press holes every ¼ inch all around photo opening. Thread a bead onto each head pin; dip pin point in glue, then press pin into hole. Repeat until all pins and beads are used.

5 Glue a feather, a piece of sea glass and a mosaic tile to lower left corner of frame; repeat at upper right corner.

6 Place photo behind frame; glue frame to front of small photo album. ◆

RUBBER STAMPS
Glass Paint
Embossing Powders
POLYMER CLAY
Metal Sheets

Give yourself permission to stamp on something other than paper. How about embossed polymer clay? Or stamped metal sheets? It's all possible, and it's all beautiful!

Southwest Accent Vase

The challenge—each designer needs to create a project using the materials we selected (and one or two more items they add).

Design by June Fiechter

Materials

- Crisa 10¾-inch-tall, 3½-inch-square glass vase from Syndicate Sales
- DC&C Tintiques 2½ x 6-inch burnished metal sign #23-1704
- Sculpey III natural-color polymer clay from Polyform Products
- ColorBox Cool Doodles Stylus Molding Mat from ClearSnap
- Ink-It 1-inch square embossing inks from Ranger Industries: clear, black
- Suze Weinberg Ultra Thick Embossing Enamels from Ranger Industries: bronze, black
- CeramDecor PermEnamel surface conditioner from Delta
- Aqua CeramDecor PermEnamel satin-finish glass paint from Delta
- CeramDecor PermEnamel clear gloss glaze from Delta
- Aqua beads
- Wire
- Craft drill with bit
- Baking sheet for clay
- Oven
- Embossing heat tool
- Glue

Instructions

1 Drill matching holes opposite the holes already in the metal sign.

2 Flatten a ball of polymer clay and press into desired pattern on molding mat. Repeat with a second ball of clay, using same pattern or different one, as desired. Trim around design areas with craft knife. Roll and flatten a plain, unpatterned piece of clay; trim edges with craft knife.

3 Bake clay panels on baking sheet according to manufacturer's instructions. Cool.

4 Using clear embossing ink, completely coat one side of metal sign. Sprinkle bronze embossing enamel over sign to cover; shake off excess. Heat sign with embossing heat tool until enamel is melted; set sign aside.

5 Clean vase and coat with surface conditioner, following manufacturer's instructions; let dry.

6 Paint vase aqua; let dry, then coat painted vase with clear gloss glaze; let dry.

7 Lightly press surface of black embossing ink pad onto cooled clay panels with patterns, touching only the raised portions of the patterns. Sprinkle black embossing enamel over clay panels; shake off excess. Heat panels with embossing heat tool until enamel is melted; set panels aside to cool.

8 Using black embossing ink pad, completely coat one side of plain clay panel. Sprinkle black embossing enamel over panel to cover; shake off excess. Heat panel with embossing heat tool until enamel is melted; set panel aside.

The possibilities of polymer clay are just endless! I found the perfect beads to match the paint colors I chose and decided on a Southwest theme for my project.
—June Fiechter

9 Paint surfaces of cooled clay panels with aqua, covering all areas that are not embossed. While still wet, wipe surface with paper towel to reveal black detailing. Let dry.

10 Wipe off surface of metal with paper towel (an oily residue will remain).

11 Glue clay pieces to front of metal sign as shown; glue beads to center panel.

12 Wire metal sign to front of vase, threading wire through holes in sign and threading beads onto ends of wire. ◆

Abstract Iris Vase

Design by Judi Kauffman

Materials

- Crisa 10¾-inch-tall, 3½-inch-square glass vase from Syndicate Sales
- DC&C Tintiques 2½ x 6-inch burnished metal sign #23-1704
- CeramDecor PermEnamel surface conditioner from Delta
- CeramDecor PermEnamel satin-finish glass paints from Delta: eggplant, Mediterranean blue, olive, tangerine, yellow
- CeramDecor PermEnamel clear gloss glaze from Delta
- ColorBox Cool Doodles Stylus Molding Mat from ClearSnap
- Ink-It black 1-inch square embossing ink from Ranger Industries
- Suze Weinberg Ultra Thick Embossing Enamels from Ranger Industries: bronze, gold
- Embossing heat tool
- Sculpey III polymer clay from Polyform Products: purple, violet, lemon
- 9 inches yellow plastic-coated 22-gauge craft wire
- Assorted round and oval beads: wood, plastic and/or glass
- ½- to ¾-inch cluster of small berries to coordinate with/complement clay colors
- Needle-nose pliers
- Wire cutters
- 2 disposable 1-inch foam paintbrushes
- Pasta machine for rolling clay or acrylic rolling pin
- Oven
- Craft cement

Painting Vase

1 Following manufacturer's instructions, clean vase, then apply surface conditioner with sponge brush. Let dry.

2 Mix 1 part olive paint with 2 parts Mediterranean blue and 4 parts yellow to make a bright olive color. Referring to photo throughout, use sponge brush to stroke long leaves onto all four sides of vase. Use side and edge of brush as well as its full width to make leaves of different widths and lengths.

3 Dry brush on paper towel but do not wash it. Use brush to add eggplant leaves to vase, painting back over and along some of the olive leaves to darken an edge or add shading. Stop before glass surfaces are completely covered; let dry.

"Sometimes a project falls into place as if by magic. The minute I saw the tall vase and jars of eggplant and olive paint (one of my favorite color combinations), I could picture slim, simple leaves reaching from end to end, the stems of long-stemmed flowers visible in the water the vase would someday contain. As soon as I painted the leaves, I began to envision a stylized marbled clay flower layered onto the surface of an embossed metal "sign" hanging on the front, a juxtaposition of textured pattern and smooth clay.

—Judi Kauffman

Continued on page 75

Craft Closet Challenge
Color Wash Vase

Design by Mary Lynn Maloney

Materials

- Crisa 10¾-inch-tall, 3½-inch-square glass vase from Syndicate Sales
- DC&C Tintiques 2½ x 6-inch burnished metal sign #23-1704
- CeramDecor PermEnamel surface conditioner from Delta
- CeramDecor PermEnamel satin-finish glass paints from Delta: eggplant, Mediterranean blue, tangerine
- CeramDecor PermEnamel clear gloss glaze from Delta
- Ink-It black 1-inch square embossing ink from Ranger Industries
- Suze Weinberg interference blue Ultra Thick Embossing Enamel from Ranger Industries
- Sculpey III polymer clay from Polyform Products: turquoise, violet
- ColorBox Cool Doodles Stylus Molding Mat from ClearSnap
- Pearl Ex powdered pigments from Jacquard: Aztec gold, interference blue, misty lavender
- Low-tack masking tape
- Soft, dry paintbrushes
- Baby powder
- Pasta machine for rolling clay *or* acrylic rolling pin
- Oven
- Embossing heat tool
- Heavy-duty scissors
- Small metal file
- Matte-finish spray sealer
- Superglue

" I was fascinated as I watched the translucent colors drizzle down the sides of this vase. It reminded me of sheets of water washing over a beach, then receding. Building up several layers of color added a very interesting texture. The soft, watery look combined with the linear tiles creates a unique contrast. "

—Mary Lynn Maloney

Instructions

1 Clean vase, then apply surface conditioner according to manufacturer's instructions. Let dry.

2 Using masking tape, create pattern of crisscrossing vertical and horizontal lines on sides of vase, pressing tape firmly into place.

3 Mix 1 part eggplant paint with 2 parts clear gloss glaze. Paint outside of vase with mixture; let dry. Remove masking tape.

4 Mix 2 tablespoons glaze with 3 drops Mediterranean blue paint. Paint over previously masked areas and eggplant areas, letting mixture drip and run down vase. Let dry.

5 Repeat step 4, but while blue paint is still wet, paint and drizzle a mixture of 1 tablespoon glaze and 1 drop tangerine paint around top edge of vase, allowing tangerine mixture to run into blue. Let dry.

6 Clean metal sign. Press black ink pad onto metal, creating nine squares. Sprinkle squares with blue embossing enamel, leaving some black ink exposed. Heat with embossing heat tool. **Note:** *Work on a heatproof surface and do not touch the metal while you heat it.* While metal is still hot, sprinkle it with additional embossing enamel and heat again. Let cool.

7 Use heavy-duty scissors to cut metal into uneven squares, leaving a margin of ⅛–¼ inch around shapes. Cut squares in two to form varying sizes of rectangles. Smooth sharp, rough edges with file.

8 Condition 1-inch ball of violet polymer clay; roll it ¼ inch thick. **Note:** *Do not use pasta machine for food preparation once you have used it with clay.* Sprinkle molding mat with a little baby powder; shake off excess. Lay mat onto clay and run both pieces through pasta machine at thickest setting. Carefully peel mat off clay. Repeat, substituting turquoise clay.

9 Cut molded violet clay into ¾- to 1-inch squares and rectangles. Repeat with molded turquoise clay. Bake pieces following manufacturer's instructions; let cool.

10 Using soft, dry paintbrush, brush turquoise squares with lavender pigment; add random brushings of gold pigment. Brush violet squares with blue pigment, then gold. Spray all pieces with two light coats matte sealer; let dry.

11 Referring to photo, position metal and clay tiles on sides of vase in a pleasing arrangement. Glue in place with superglue. ◆

Abstract Iris Vase
Continued from page 73

4 Seal sides of vase with two coats clear gloss glaze.

Iris Ornament

1 Mask center area of burnished metal sign by taping a piece of paper across it at an angle.

2 Lay molding mat texture side up on a piece of paper. Use ink pad to apply embossing ink to surface of mat. Press metal sign onto inked surface to stamp pattern onto it. Do not let metal slide; lift it straight up.

3 While ink is still wet, sprinkle gold embossing enamel across top section of sign only (top has holes along edge); shake off excess and return it to jar. Sprinkle bronze embossing enamel across bottom section; shake off excess. Carefully remove masking paper from center of sign. Using embossing heat tool, heat and melt powders.

4 *Hanger:* Thread desired beads onto wire; thread ends through holes in sign and twist to secure.

5 Mix three colors of clay in pasta machine or blend them by hand to make a marbled blend; do not overblend. **Note:** *Do not use pasta machine for food once it has been used with clay.* Select the most interesting areas of clay, and from them, roll two large, flat, oval petals. Pinch petals together at center and twist ends. Roll three smaller oval petals; fold one in half. Attach these to top of larger ovals with folded petal at top.

6 From marbled clay, roll two 3-inch "snakes"; twist into a spiral and attach to flower as shown, pressing with finger to make small indentation at center. Bake clay pieces following manufacturer's instructions; let cool.

7 Glue small berry cluster bead at center of flower. Glue flower to metal sign; let glue dry. Hang on front of vase. ◆

Summer Evening Candle Votive

While fun to look at in the daylight, this votive candle really comes alive at night.

Design by Lisa Galvin

Materials

- 3-inch-square, 3½-inch-tall square glass votive
- Soft polymer clay: caramel, chocolate, tan, copper, cognac, black
- Medium-weight copper embossing sheet
- Ink pad for stamping on metal
- Copper embossing powder
- Embossing heat gun
- Acrylic roller *or* brayer for clay
- 1⅛ x 1-inch dragonfly paper punch
- Rubber stamps: 1 x 1¼-inch ladybug, insect wings
- Red glass/tile paint
- Paintbrush
- 18-gauge annealed wire
- Pebbles
- Round-nose pliers
- Floating candle
- Foil
- Fine-point black permanent marking pen for nonporous surfaces
- Permanent glass/gem adhesive
- Wire cutters
- Craft knife
- 4-inch ceramic tiles
- Baking sheet for clay
- Waxed paper
- Tape
- Scrap paper

When blended together, bits and pieces of polymer clay left from other projects create swirling stonelike effects that are never the same. Inspired by my love of gardening and the outdoors, this design seemed to come to life on its own!

—Lisa Galvin

Base & Cattails

1 Working with small balls of clay and starting with lightest colors, knead individual colors to condition them, making clay more pliable. Blend colors together, twisting, turning and tearing until desired effect is achieved. Do not work with it too much or the clay will blend into a solid color, diminishing the final mottled effect. You will need a fist-size ball of mottled clay to complete the project. Flatten blended clay into a thick pancake between your palms.

2 *Base:* To conserve clay and make the base lighter, crumple aluminum foil and form it into a tight, flattened square ³⁄₁₆ inch thick; its outer dimensions should match the measurement of the bottom of the glass votive.

3 Lay foil square on work surface covered with waxed paper. Stack two 4-inch tiles to right of foil square, leaving 1 inch between tiles and foil (these serve as guides for rolling the clay). Repeat on left side of foil. Center clay pancake over top of foil; roll with acrylic roller until outer edges of roller

come to rest on tiles. This will leave a thin, even sheet of clay over top of foil.

4 Place glass votive in center and press down to indent slightly; mark size needed and placement location. Roll again lightly. Trim edges of base in an uneven, natural shape, allowing a margin of ¾–1¼ inches between votive and edge. Smooth cut edges.

5 Condition and roll black clay to make a ¼-inch-thick bottom for base. Place blended clay on top of black, rolling it to adhere, and trim black clay with craft knife to match shape of blended base.

6 Cut seven or more 3-inch pieces of wire; insert into clay base at corners where cattails will be positioned later. Place base on baking sheet.

7 *Cattails:* Roll remaining bits of blended clay into a rope. Cut four 1-inch pieces, threading each lengthwise onto a 7-inch piece of wire. Arrange clay so that when wire is placed crosswise on oven rack, clay is suspended between wires of rack.

8 Bake clay base and cattails as directed by manufacturer; let cool. Remove 3-inch wires from base; these wires can now be discarded.

9 Leaving them on wire on which they were baked, roll cattails on ink pad; sprinkle with embossing powder and heat to emboss. Do not burn. Let cool.

10 Remove cattails from wire; slip onto new wire pieces cut at random lengths. Use round-nose pliers to curl a loop at one end (top) of each cattail; slip straight ends into prepared holes on clay base. Place a drop of glue at base of cattail to hold it in place; let dry.

Votive

1 Stamp ladybug on a small piece of scrap paper; insert inside votive and tape in place to use as guide for painting wings on outside of votive with red tile paint. Follow paint manufacturer's instructions regarding application, use and drying time. Repeat to paint wings on all sides of votive, varying position of ladybugs. Let dry completely.

2 Align and stamp ladybugs on top of wings. See manufacturer's instructions to check if ink needs to be heat-set. Touch up dry designs as needed with permanent black pen.

3 Punch four dragonflies from copper embossing sheet. Place on baking sheet; heat with embossing heat gun to change color tones; let cool.

4 Ink wing-pattern rubber stamp with embossing ink and press onto dragonflies' wings; sprinkle with embossing powder and tap off excess. Heat with gun to emboss.

5 Using permanent marking pen, add stripes to dragonfly bodies. Glue dragonflies to sides of votive as shown.

6 Place votive on vase. Glue pebbles at corners of base; votive should fit between them snugly, but should be able to be removed easily.

7 Fill votive two-thirds full with water; add floating candle. ◆

Create

Substitute star punches to make starfish, painted fish motifs for the ladybugs, and aquarium gravel for the pebbles to make a fun underwater scene.

Ladybug Suncatcher

Hang this fun accent in a window where the sun can reflect from the shimmery metal dangles.

Design by Sherian Frey

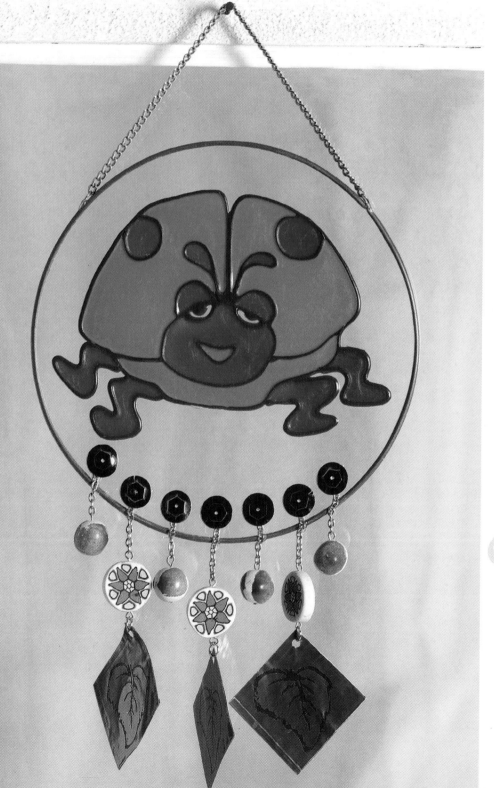

Materials

- 6-inch glass circle with chain for hanging
- Surface conditioner
- Glass paints: red, blue
- Black liquid stained glass leading
- Leaf rubber stamp
- White polymer clay
- Starflower polymer clay millefiori cane
- Blue embossing powder
- 7 silver flathead pins *or* eye pins
- Red metal embossing sheet
- Blue metal paint
- 3 silver jump rings
- Metal chain to match hanging chain on suncatcher
- 7 (10mm) red sequins
- Waterproof, weatherproof, clear craft cement
- Needle-nose pliers
- Glass cleaner
- Felt-tip pen
- Small flat paintbrush
- ⅛-inch round hole punch
- Sharp blade

I was in the mood for fun and whimsy when I created this project, and I enjoy working with paints that have a stained glass effect. Since the paint, metal and polymer clay are all waterproof, this whimsical ladybug can decorate your window or garden with a touch of cheery color and fun.

—Sherian Frey

Instructions

1 Clean glass and apply surface conditioner as required by paint manufacturer.

2 Place pattern under glass; trace outlines with liquid leading (do not trace dots at bottom). Let dry.

3 Referring to photo throughout, fill in sections of design with glass paints; let dry.

4 Shape four ½-inch balls of white polymer clay. Insert flathead pin through center of each. Holding both ends of pin, dip clay ball into blue embossing powder leaving a white ½-inch-wide strip through center. (Use pins to support balls during baking so that embossing powder does not touch anything.)

5 From clay millefiori cane, cut three ⅛-inch slices with a sharp blade. Insert flathead pin though center diameter of each slice (from side to side of slice); hold clay gently but firmly between thumb and forefinger as pin is inserted through edge to keep side of disc from flattening out where pin is inserted. Pin will remain in clay slice.

6 Bake balls and millefiori slices as directed by manufacturer; let cool. Snug pinhead against each ball and trim other end to ¼ inch; form ring in cut end with needle-nose pliers. Cut ends of pins in millefiori discs to ¼ inch; use pliers to make loops in pin ends.

7 From red metal embossing sheet, cut 1¾-inch square and 1½-inch square. Center smaller square on larger one, silver sides facing; secure with a dot of cement. Scribe fold line on larger square along edges of smaller square; fold edges to enclose smaller square. Crease folds sharply using the side of a pencil. Repeat to make a total of three red metal squares.

8 Using rubber stamp and metal paint as ink, print design on finished squares. Let dry.

9 Punch hole in one corner of each square; add jump ring. Attach each square to one of the millefiori discs, linking jump ring on square and wire loop on disc.

10 Using cement, glue seven 1-inch lengths of chain across bottom of glass suncatcher where indicated by dots. Lay project flat for gluing; let dry undisturbed for 1 hour.

11 Embed glued end of each chain in a bead of glue slightly larger than ⅛ inch; press sequin into glue. Let dry.

12 Attach embossed ball ornaments and millefiori/metal dangles to ends of chains. ◆

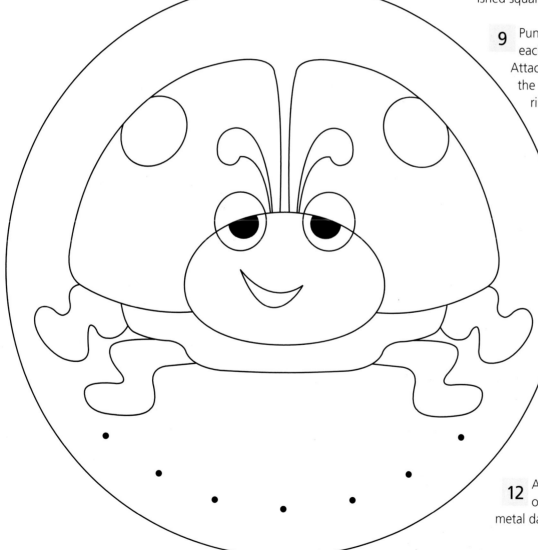

Ladybug Suncatcher

Verdigris Leaves Miniature Chimenea

Coppery clay leaves and a mosaic border give an Aztec look to this clay candleholder.

Design by Sandy L. Rollinger

Materials
- 10-inch terra-cotta chimenea
- Terra-cotta polymer clay
- Translucent liquid polymer clay
- Leaf rubber stamp
- Clear embossing ink
- Verdigris embossing powder
- Embossing heat tool
- 2 x 10-inch strip cut from copper sheet
- Dark green stained glass paint
- Small all-purpose craft brush
- Small paintbrush
- Lucite brayer *or* rolling pin for clay
- Craft knife
- Toothpick
- Freezer paper
- Foil-lined cookie sheet
- Oven
- Tea-light candle

Instructions

1 Referring to package instructions, condition clay. Cover protective cutting surface with freezer paper. Place one section of clay on top; roll and flatten to ⅛-inch thickness. Using a sharp craft knife, cut two strips of clay ½ inch wide and long enough to go around top and side opening of chimenea.

2 Referring to photo throughout, use a small brush to apply liquid clay around edges of chimenea; press strips into place. Using handle of craft knife, indent circles 1 inch apart all along clay strips.

3 Cut small triangles from copper. Apply dots of liquid clay to strips between indented circles and press triangles into place. Using a toothpick, indent vertical lines between the circles and triangles.

4 Using rubber stamp, press 10–12 leaf images onto remaining flattened clay; cut out each with a craft knife. Apply a little liquid clay on bottom right area of chimenea; press leaf in place, slightly overlapping opening as shown. Continue adding more leaves as shown, working upward and curving around side opening toward center, until you reach the top. Bend and mold leaves for a natural shape.

5 Set chimenea on foil-lined cookie sheet; bake in preheated oven according to instructions for clay. Let cool in oven before moving.

6 Use a small paintbrush to apply clear embossing ink to leaves' edges and veins. Pour embossing powder over freshly inked surfaces. Add ink and embossing powder to clay areas on strips around side opening and top, avoiding the indented circles (step 2). Use heat tool to emboss powder.

7 Fill indented circles with dark green glass paint; let dry. Place tea-light candle inside chimenea. ◆

Nature inspired this project. I wanted to create something for the outdoors on my patio, and several of these will create a nice atmosphere for evening festivities. Adding a citronella tea-light candle helps keep away unwanted guests, too.

—Sandy L. Rollinger

Botanical Garden Box

Stamped ceramic tiles are softly colored with stamping inks.

Design by Chris Malone

Materials
- 10-inch wooden window box
- 3 (3-inch) white ceramic tiles
- 1 ounce white polymer clay
- Gold metal embossing sheet
- Rubber stamps: floral collage, small leaves
- Ink pads: black pigment, soft green dye-based
- Black embossing powder
- Embossing heat tool
- Glass paints: yellow, orange, pink, blue, lavender, green
- Clear gloss sealer
- Sandpaper
- Spray matte finish
- Painters' tape
- Cosmetic sponges *or other small sponge applicators*
- Paintbrush
- Zigzag pattern-edge scissors
- Stylus *or ballpoint pen*
- Silicone glue *or superglue*
- Palette

The addition of ceramic tiles brought this project together for me. Tiles, clay and foil are all suitable for decorating a wooden box, and a floral theme seemed appropriate for a window box that could hold small pots of flowers or green plants.

—**Chris Malone**

Box

1 Sand box; wipe off dust. Spray box with two or three coats matte finish inside and out, letting finish dry between coats.

2 Blend 1 part blue glass paint with 3 parts clear gloss sealer; brush mixture onto section of box and immediately wipe off with paper towel or rag to stain wood a light blue. Repeat until all surfaces of box are stained; apply a second coat if more intense color is preferred.

Tiles

1 Clean and dry ceramic tiles.

2 If stamp is larger than tiles, use painters' tape to mask edges of

Continued on page 91

Dressed-Up Terra-Cotta Pot

Accent plain pots with fancy labels embellished with texturized metal plates.

Design by Mary Lynn Maloney

Materials
- 4⅛-inch-tall, 4¾-inch-diameter terra-cotta flowerpot with saucer
- Blue frosted-finish glass paint
- Blue-gold iridescent acrylic paint
- 1-inch ball pearl polymer clay
- Embossing powders: copper, verdigris
- ½-inch alphabet rubber stamp set
- Black waterproof archival stamp pad
- Brass metal embossing sheet
- Copper metal mesh sheet
- Pasta machine for rolling clay *or* acrylic rolling pin
- Gem glue
- Superglue
- ⅛-inch round hole punch
- Embossing punch
- Paintbrushes
- Large rubber bands

Instructions

1 Referring to photo throughout, use blue frosted paint and ½-inch brush to paint vertical stripes around rim of pot. Paint saucer's rim with small dots of blue frosted paint. Let dry.

2 Paint a blue-gold iridescent dot in center of each stripe on top

Planted with the appropriate herb, one of these elegantly embellished clay pots would make a very thoughtful gift for a gardener. Or make a gift basket by putting in a pot, a small bag of potting soil and some seeds.
—**Mary Lynn Maloney**

of pot rim. Paint entire base of saucer with blue-gold; let dry. Add another coat of blue-gold to saucer if necessary.

3 Warm and condition polymer clay in your hands; roll it ¼ inch thick. **Note:** *Do not use pasta machine for food preparation once you have used it with clay.*

4 Sprinkle surface of clay with a pinch of copper embossing powder, then a pinch of verdigris. Roll and twist clay to work powders into clay (they will add sparkle and texture to clay once it is baked). Repeat.

5 Roll clay ⅛ inch thick. Using black ink and alphabet stamps,

stamp the word "dill" (or word of your choice) into clay; let dry.

6 Using craft knife, cut the clay into an irregular shape, following the lines of the stamped letters. Bake clay following manufacturer's instructions; let cool.

7 Paint edges of clay with blue-gold paint. While paint is still wet, dip edges into copper embossing powder, then heat with embossing tool until raised effect occurs.

8 Place clay panel onto brass metal sheet. Cut an irregular rectangle from brass metal sheet that is ⅜–½ inch larger all around than

clay. Use embossing punch to add texture to the metal. Brush surface with a very small amount of blue-gold paint; let dry.

9 Place brass rectangle on top of copper mesh. Cut mesh ¼ inch larger all around; fold excess mesh over onto front of brass. Using hole punch, punch three holes, evenly spaced, down left and right edges of assembled metal piece.

10 Use gem glue to glue clay panel in center of metal piece.

11 Glue clay-and-metal panel to side of pot with superglue, gently coaxing the panel to conform to curve of pot. Hold panel in place with several large rubber bands until glue dries. ◆

Fantasy Fairy Doll

Since the body of this cute little doll is premade, you'll have lots of time to add fun embellishments.

Design by Samantha McNesby

Materials
- Glass paints: white with glitter, blue, lavender, green, purple
- Light blue embossing powder
- Scraps of polymer clay: blue, green, white
- 1 brass embossing sheet
- Rubber stamp with allover bamboo or leaf pattern
- Assorted glass seed beads in blue, teal and green
- White ready-made fabric art doll
- Foam brush
- Scruffy paintbrush
- Rolling pin *or* pasta machine for clay
- Foil-covered baking sheet
- Oven
- 1-inch star cookie cutter
- Needle and thread
- Paper
- Cement glue

Painting Doll

1 Work next to sink or other water source; wear plastic gloves, if desired. Wet hands thoroughly. Run wet hands all over the doll, dampening it thoroughly.

2 Pour a quarter-size puddle of white glitter glass paint into the palm of your hand and rub your hands together. Run your paint-covered hands all over the doll, covering it completely.

3 Before paint dries and without cleaning your hands, immediately repeat the painting process with a dime-size puddle of blue paint. Let the blue blend with the white, and leave some white showing.

4 Immediately repeat painting process with a dime-size puddle of lavender paint, letting some of the blue paint show through. Let paints dry.

Stamping Doll

1 Using foam brush, apply blue glass paint to rubber stamp. Stamp image all over doll, adding more paint as needed.

2 Repeat stamping process using green paint, then purple, using as much or as little of each color as you like.

3 While stamped images are still wet, sprinkle doll with light blue embossing powder; let dry completely. Once doll is dry, shake off excess embossing powder.

Marbled Clay Buttons

1 Roll ½-inch ball of white polymer clay and another of green; shape each into a 3-inch snake approximately ¼ inch thick. Lay snakes side by side and press together lightly. Gently twist snakes together, creating a spiral.

2 Roll clay spiral into a ball; then, form ball into a snake, and twist to blend the colors. Continue blending until you achieve the desired effect; do not over-blend or you will lose the marbled effect.

3 Repeat steps 1 and 2 with white and blue clays.

4 Using pasta machine or rolling pin, roll marbled clay ⅛ inch thick. Cut a star from each color using cookie cutter.

5 Place stars on foil-covered baking sheet and bake according to manufacturer's instructions. Remove from oven; let cool.

Wings

1 Make paper patterns for wings, sketching a squatty, pointed, 1¾ x 2½-inch teardrop shape for top wings and a longer, 1¾ x 4-inch teardrop for bottom wings. Cut two of each pattern from brass embossing sheet.

2 Using scruffy paintbrush, dab wings with blue, purple and white paints; let dry.

3 Referring to photo throughout, cement larger bottom wings in

An art doll like this one is a great project to use up those leftover bits and pieces in your workroom. Gather small items that are in the same color family, select some paints to match, and you are on your way. Use a premade doll form so you can start painting and embellishing right away.

—Samantha McNesby

place on back of doll, points touching. Add smaller top wings. Let cement dry.

Accents

1 *Fringe hair:* Thread needle with 1 yard thread; tie knot. Add beaded fringe along top of doll's head, stringing beads randomly to make ½- to 1-inch strands of fringe: String on desired number of beads, then take needle back through second to last bead and all remaining beads on that strand. Take needle down into head and bring out at position of next strand of fringe; repeat. When you reach the end, knot thread to secure.

2 *Anklets:* Thread needle with 1 yard thread; tie knot. Bring thread out at back of ankle; string on enough beads to go around ankle; take thread back in at back of ankle and knot. Repeat on second ankle.

3 Glue clay buttons to front of doll; let glue dry completely. ◆

Oriental Wisdom Altered Book

Altered books are all the rage, and this Asian-influenced example makes a great decorating accent.

Design by Katie Hacker

Materials
- Hardbound book with blank cover and strong spine
- Rubber stamps: "Long Life" and "Long Life" with border, Chinese coin, Chinese calligraphy, Chinese character "Fortune," "Friend" and "Joy" stamps, Celtic and classic alphabet stamps
- Metallic pigment ink pads for stamping on metal: copper, black
- 9¼ x 12-inch sheet medium-weight copper
- 3 x 5-inch piece glass with beveled edge (salvaged from picture frame)
- Black polymer clay
- Copper buffing medium
- Copper embossing powder
- Embossing gel
- Embossing heat tool
- Black card stock *or* heavy paper
- Black glass paint
- ¼-inch hole punch
- ¼-inch copper eyelets
- 2 (4¼ x 7⅜-inch) pieces copper mesh
- Glue stick
- Craft glue
- Craft cement
- Tape
- Paintbrushes: small round, medium flat
- Drinking glass
- Baby powder
- Baking sheet or oven-proof plate
- Scrap paper
- Oven

I took one look at this hardbound book at my local discount store and knew I had to have it. The black cover was a perfect base for stamping and I was intrigued by the title, Mandarin Plaid. I decided to go with the Asian theme and give the novel a new lease on life. You can choose any theme for your own altered book. Let the title be your inspiration!

—Katie Hacker

Cover

1 Referring to photo throughout, stamp front cover of book with assorted images using copper pigment ink and a variety of Chinese motifs.

2 Cut 3 x 5-inch piece from copper sheet; place on scrap paper and stamp all over metal with Chinese characters using black ink pad. Let dry. Glue stamped copper panel to front cover.

3 Referring to paint manufacturer's instructions, paint a black band freehand along edges of glass; let dry. Glue glass on top of copper, applying a thin bead of craft cement along each edge.

4 Roll a 2-inch ball of black clay; using the bottom of a drinking glass, press it into a disc ¼ inch thick. Sprinkle baby powder over the "long life" stamp; shake off excess and press stamp firmly into clay, making a deep impression; remove stamp.

5 Roll four ¼-inch balls of clay; use your finger to flatten them into discs.

6 Place all clay pieces on baking sheet or ovenproof plate and bake them following manufacturer's instructions; let cool.

7 Following manufacturer's instructions, use small round paintbrush to apply copper buffing medium to recessed areas of clay "long life" character, leaving black raised lines visible. Glue image in center of glass plate.

8 Cover top of each small disc with embossing gel, then coat with copper embossing powder. Heat with embossing heat tool; let cool. Glue discs in corners of glass plate as shown.

2 Rub black ink pad onto outer edges of all pages on the spread, and stamp pages randomly with black Chinese images.

3 Cut 1¾ x 8-inch strip from copper sheet; glue it along left edge of first (left-facing page) in spread.

4 Cut a 1¼ x 8-inch strip of black paper; using Chinese character stamp(s) and copper ink pad, stamp images on paper strip. Glue it to copper strip, slightly off-center, as shown.

5 Cut several ½-inch-wide strips from copper sheet. Using Celtic alphabet stamps and black ink, stamp "the journey/of a/thousand miles/ begins with/a single/step/— lao tzu." Cut strips apart where indicated and glue across foldout as shown.

6 Connect the copper panels with ¼-inch strips cut from black paper and glued to the pages.

Stair-Step Spread

1 Lay a ruler along center of open book and use craft knife to cut along its edge through as many pages as desired (six pages on sample project). Move ruler out so that it lies along cut edge of these pages, and cut through another section of pages. Move ruler out again and repeat; continuing to cut pages in stair-step fashion as desired. (It is not necessary to

Endpapers

1 Stamp inside front and back covers with assorted images using black pigment ink and a variety of Chinese motifs.

2 Cut 2 x 3½-inch piece from copper sheet. Using black ink pad and Celtic alphabet stamps, stamp "dedicated to the travelers" or phrase of your choice onto copper; stamp a Chinese image below the lettering. Let dry, then glue in bottom left-hand corner inside front cover.

3 Using hole punch, punch through top and bottom outer corners of first 10–12 pages of book. Set an eyelet in each hole to hold pages together.

Foldout Spread

1 Carefully cut two pages out of book. Use adhesive tape to attach them side by side to another page in the book. Leave a little space where you join them so that can easily be folded up accordion style.

Create

Instead of Oriental stamps, substitute musical notes and heart motifs to make a romantic altered book.

glue sections of pages together.)

2. Rub top page of each section with black ink to give it an antiqued appearance; let dry,

3. Cut four ¼- to ½-inch-wide strips from copper sheet, as long as pages are tall; glue one near edge of top sheet in each section as shown.

4. Stamp copper Chinese characters on black paper; let dry. Cut paper into three ¼-inch-wide strips and glue to top pages of three center sections, between edge of page and copper strip.

5. Cover facing pages of stair-step section with black paper. Stamp copper "long life" medallion in center of first (left-facing) page; let dry.

6. Beginning with right-facing page at end of stair steps, hold the next 10–12 pages together and punch through top and bottom outer corners with hole punch. Set eyelet in each hole to hold those pages together. Trim black paper from around eyelets as shown.

Ribbon-Bound Spread

1. Rub copper and black ink pads over two facing pages to give them an antiqued appearance; let dry.

2. Glue a piece of wire mesh over each page as shown.

3. Cut two 1¼ x 6-inch strips black paper. Leave ½ inch blank on left end of strip; then, using Celtic alphabet stamps and copper ink, stamp "wherever you go," on strip. Leave ½ inch blank on right end of remaining strip, and beginning on left end, stamp "go with all your heart."

4. Glue paper strip with first half of quote across top third of left-facing page, folding blank end under and wrapping it around the preceding pages (10 or 12 on sample). This gives the appearance of a ribbon-bound package. Glue second half of quote just below center of right-facing page, wrapping the blank portion over the edge of the next 10–12 pages.

5. Cut a ½ x 2½-inch strip of black paper; using Celtic alphabet stamps and copper ink, stamp "—Confucius" onto it. Let dry, then glue stamped strip in lower right portion of right-facing page as shown.

Spine

Cut a ¾ x 8-inch strip of black paper; using uppercase classic alphabet stamps and copper ink, stamp "TRAVEL WISDOM" (or title of your choice) and your initials onto it. Let dry, then glue strip to spine. ◆

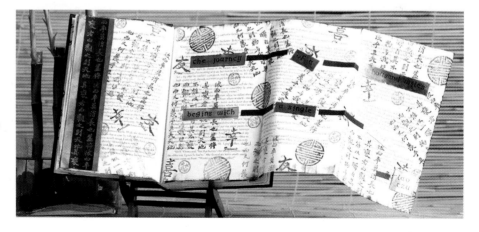

Copper Accent Jewelry Set

Carefully formed metal shapes serve as accents and backdrops for elegant clay jewelry.

Design by Vicki Schreiner

Materials

- Pink pearl polymer clay
- Copper embossing sheet
- Transparent glass paints: rose, white
- Background stamps: crackle, acanthus
- Embossing pad
- Embossing powder: white, sparkle
- Embossing heat tool
- Glass/metal cement
- Razor blade
- Stylus
- Brass jewelry bail
- Hook earring with spacer beads
- Self-adhesive pin backs
- Rolling pin
- Waxed paper
- Cookie sheet
- Metal spatula
- Masking tape
- Round #3 paintbrush
- Small nail or pushpin
- Hammer
- Needle-nose pliers
- Black fine-point permanent marker
- Flat plastic cut from empty milk jug, coffee can lid or stencil sheet
- Palette
- Sheet of plain white paper

Preparing Clay

1 Preheat oven to 275 degrees Fahrenheit. Place clay ball between two sheets of waxed paper on work surface; roll clay ⅛ inch thick with rolling pin. Peel off top waxed paper sheet.

2 Using razor blade and ruler, cut 1-inch-wide strip of clay. From this strip, cut a piece 1¾ inches long for pin and a 1-inch square for pendant. From remaining clay, cut two ½-inch squares for earrings.

3 Place pieces in center of cookie sheet. Bake for 15 minutes; do not overbake. Set aside to cool.

Cutting & Embossing Copper

1 Using patterns as templates, trace each pattern onto copper sheet and plastic as directed using fine-point marker; cut out with scissors.

2 Using stylus and ruler, score pieces where indicated by dashed lines, running stylus back and forth along ruler to indent copper.

3 *Assemble backs:* Place plastic backing

Trying my hand at metal was a treat! I thought that it would be a good idea to start with something small, and jewelry came to mind. I quickly discovered how fast and easy metal is to work with. Metal, polymer clay and embossing are the perfect combination for creating classy accessories with style!

—**Vicki Schreiner**

Vary the clay and metal colors to create stylistic pieces that match any outfit in your wardrobe—from casual to classic!

Create

onto metal backing and press down firmly to flatten (plastic is now sandwiched between copper pieces). Using small nail or pushpin and hammer, add a small hole through pendant and earrings where indicated.

4 Lay stamps on counter, rubber up. Using embossing pad, generously apply ink to area of stamp you wish to use.

Earrings and pendant: Place piece facedown onto inked area of stamp and press straight down without rocking; remove. Reload stamp with ink for each piece.

Pin: Place masking tape diagonally across bottom of piece, allowing room for ⅜-inch striped area across middle. Apply ink to exposed area as instructed for earrings and pendant.

5 Lay each stamped piece on plain white paper. Shake on white embossing powder to cover stamped area; turn each piece upside down and tap to remove excess. Place pieces on cookie sheet. Use heat tool to emboss each piece, following manufacturer's instructions. Let cool.

Pin: After embossing and cooling top half, remove masking tape. Apply new piece of tape over embossed

piece on center of corresponding scored copper piece and top with matching copper backing piece. Carefully fold scored edges over

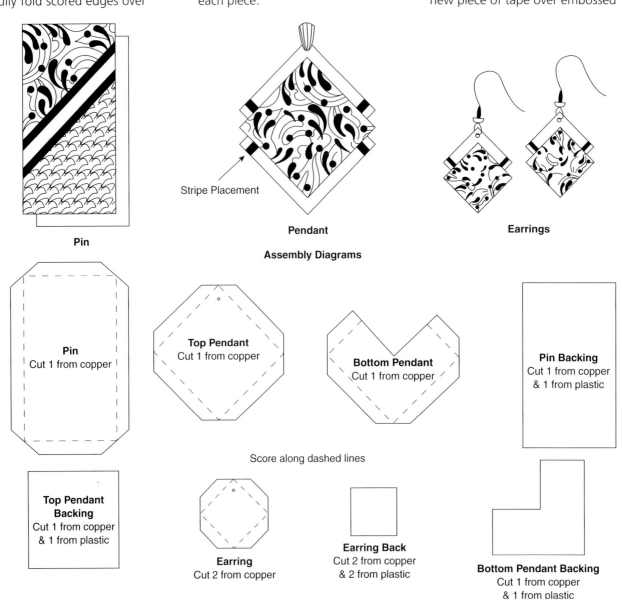

Pin

Stripe Placement

Pendant

Assembly Diagrams

Earrings

Pin
Cut 1 from copper

Top Pendant
Cut 1 from copper

Bottom Pendant
Cut 1 from copper

Pin Backing
Cut 1 from copper
& 1 from plastic

Score along dashed lines

Top Pendant Backing
Cut 1 from copper
& 1 from plastic

Earring
Cut 2 from copper

Earring Back
Cut 2 from copper
& 2 from plastic

Bottom Pendant Backing
Cut 1 from copper
& 1 from plastic

area. Apply ink to bottom half of pin using alternate stamp pad and sparkle embossing powder. Use heat tool to complete embossing; let cool.

Painting

1 Pour small puddle of rose transparent glass paint on palette. Using paintbrush, randomly add comma strokes and dots to embossed areas of each clay piece as desired. Let dry. Paint ⅜-inch-wide strip diagonally across middle of pin; let dry.

2 Pour small puddle of white glass paint on palette. Using paintbrush, add small stripe to front of each metal piece as shown in diagrams; let dry.

Assembly

1 Using glass/metal cement, glue pieces together as shown in assembly diagrams. Before assembling pin, cut a metal strip 2 x ³/₁₆ inch; wrap around pin on the diagonal down middle of painted stripe. Attach ends on back with cement; let dry.

2 Attach bail to pendant; pinch closed with needle-nose pliers. Thread necklace chain through bail. Peel backing from self-adhesive pin back and press in place on back of pin. Using needle-nose pliers, open eye on each earring hook; slide earring piece onto eye and close carefully. ◆

Botanical Garden Box
Continued from page 81

tiles. (On sample project, ¾-inch painters' tape was cut in half and applied to allow a ⅜-inch border around edges of tiles.)

3 Apply black pigment ink to stamp; stamp onto tile. If using a large background stamp, as was used on the sample, a different area of the stamp can be applied to each tile.

4 Before ink dries, sprinkle tiles with embossing powder. Tap off excess, then melt powder with embossing tool and let cool to complete the embossed effect. Let dry.

5 Pour small puddles of each color paint on palette; blend a few drops of gloss sealer into each color to make paints more translucent. Pat paints onto tiles with sponge applicators or fingers. Paint dries quickly; add more paint if darker areas are desired. Let dry.

6 Brush painted tiles with gloss sealer; remove tape and let dry completely.

Clay Panels

1 Following manufacturer's instructions, condition a ½-ounce piece of white clay and form it into a small egg. Roll clay into an irregular oval ⅛ inch thick. Repeat to make a second oval.

2 Press small leaf stamp straight down into clay, without rocking. Lift up stamp. Repeat on second oval; bake clay pieces according to manufacturer's instructions.

3 Brush gloss sealer over raised surface of clay pieces; let dry.

4 Using sponge applicator, lightly color leaf imprints with soft green ink; let dry.

Assembly

1 Using regular scissors, cut two pieces, 1½ x 2½ inches, from gold sheet. Trim edges with zigzag scissors. These pieces will be glued to the front of the box, under the tiles, leaving a center section of gold visible (refer to photo throughout).

2 Lay gold pieces facedown on a soft surface such as a pad of paper, and use a stylus or pen to cover the center area with small curlicues. No smooth surface should be visible once tiles and gold pieces are glued in place.

Create Use alphabet stamps and pastel colors to make a neat organizer for a baby's room.

3 Center three tiles on long side of box; insert gold embossed shapes between tiles and glue all pieces in place as shown; let dry.

4 Using regular scissors, cut two rectangles from remaining gold sheet, each about 1 inch larger than clay leaf panels. Trim edges with zigzag scissors. These pieces will be glued to ends of box under clay panels.

5 Referring to step 2, emboss outer areas of gold pieces with curlicues. Again, no smooth surface should be visible once clay panels are glued in center.

6 Glue a gold piece and clay panel to each end of box as shown; let dry. ◆

JEWELS & GEMS
Stencils
Stamping Ink Pads

Ink pads are naturals for stencil projects—whether you stencil with them directly or transfer the ink to a brush. It dries quickly and is perfect for stenciling on paper. When you have finished stenciling, add gemstones for a touch of sparkle.

Simple Flower Chest of Drawers

The challenge—each designer needs to create a project using the materials we selected (and one or two more items they add).

Design by June Fiechter

Usually stamp pads are not compatible with a slick surface like these cardboard drawers, so at first I was apprehensive when I saw the products for this chapter challenge. However, these stamping inks are absolutely awesome! They dry quickly and remain bright in color. I originally wanted to use the entire drawer front for designing, but I decided to keep them simple so I opted for a single flower in the corners. I was concerned about the size of the pebbles stealing the show so I used only one in the center of each drawer. I'm looking forward to using this project to organize my work area.

—June Fiechter

Materials

- Highsmith Colorful Corruboard black mini shelf #Q43-26195 with six drawers #Q43-26196
- Classic Dimensions tea rose stencil #CDS-3 from American Traditional Stencils
- Peacock Billiance Archival Pigment "rainbow" ink pad from Tsukineko
- Tsukineko sponge dauber
- Ice-clear Rox from Judi-Kins
- Diamond Glaze Dimensional Adhesive from Judi-Kins
- 6 clear Glass Picture Pebbles from Judi-Kins
- 12 fuchsia crystals #5520 from Creative Crystal Co.
- Bejeweler Rhinestone Applicator from Creative Crystal Co.

Instructions

1 Referring to photo throughout, assemble shelves according to manufacturer's instructions; lay unit on level surface, face up.

2 Lay stencil to position small flower with leaf at one side of a drawer front; use dauber and ink pad to stencil flower and leaf, applying several coats as needed. Repeat to stencil a flower with leaf on each side of each drawer front. Let dry.

3 Using rhinestone applicator, attach a fuchsia crystal in center of each flower.

4 Apply a thin layer of adhesive directly from bottle onto stenciled leaves and flowers, avoiding rhine-stone centers. While still wet, sprinkle with ice-clear Rox. Let dry, then tap off excess. Repeat to cover all flowers with Rox.

5 Use adhesive to attach one pebble to center of each drawer front for pull. ◆

Japanese Garden Chest of Drawers

Design by Judi Kauffman

Instructions

1 Referring to photo throughout, assemble shelves and drawers according to manufacturer's instructions.

2 Using mineral ink pad as applicator, randomly apply ink to fronts of drawers and exterior of chest; let dry.

This was another very enjoyable challenge. I liked the shiny black surface of the chest and originally planned to do collage only on the drawer fronts, but then the black exterior looked bland so I added color to the whole thing. With a mottled surface, if there's ever a scratch or stain, I can easily sponge on more ink to repair the surface. I selected a single swirl from the stencil because I wanted to create the look of a Japanese kimono fabric, and that section of the stencil was just right.

—Judi Kauffman

3 Mask areas around swirl at top right of stencil. Use stencil dauber and blue section of peacock ink pad to add swirls of color to drawer fronts as shown or as desired. Let dry.

4 Use adhesive to attach blue, green and purple picture pebbles to leaf and flower sections of origami paper. (Reserve remaining pebbles for another project.) When glue is dry, cut off excess paper around each pebble.

5 Use adhesive to attach flower beads and paper-backed pebbles singly, in pairs or in clusters of three or more close to stenciled swirls so that they appear to be "growing" along curved stems; let dry.

6 Using rhinestone applicator and following manufacturer's instructions, attach rhinestones on stenciled swirls and clustered near or below pebbles and flower beads.

7 Draw additional freehand swirls on drawers with liquid glaze; immediately sprinkle with turquoise Rox. Let dry, then tap off excess. ◆

Materials

- Highsmith Colorful Corruboard black mini shelf #Q43-26195 with six drawers #Q43-26196
- Classic Dimensions tea rose stencil #CDS-3 from American Traditional Stencils
- Billiance Archival Pigment "rainbow" ink pads from Tsukineko: mineral, peacock
- Tsukineko sponge daubers
- Turquoise Rox from Judi-Kins
- Diamond Glaze Dimensional Adhesive from Judi-Kins
- Multicolored Glass Picture Pebbles from Judi-Kins
- Jet AB Austrian crystals #5523 from Creative Crystal Co.
- Bejeweler Rhinestone Applicator from Creative Crystal Co.
- Blue-and-white flower-pattern origami paper
- Pink/purple ¼-inch flower beads

Spring Blossoms Chest of Drawers

Design by Mary Lynn Maloney

Materials

- Highsmith Colorful Corruboard black mini shelf #Q43-26195 with six drawers #Q43-26196
- Classic Dimensions tea rose stencil #CDS-3 from American Traditional Stencils
- Billiance Archival Pigment "rainbow" ink pads from Tsukineko: twilight, peacock
- Tsukineko sponge daubers
- Rox from Judi-Kins: turquoise, amethyst, rose quartz
- Diamond Glaze Dimensional Adhesive from Judi-Kins
- Glass Picture Pebbles from Judi-Kins: 3 light blue, 3 light rose
- Yuzen Chiyogami paper in assorted pastels from Aitoh Origami Paper
- 6 (¼-inch) jet black/blue rhinestones
- Bejeweler Rhinestone Applicator from Creative Crystal Co.
- 3 x 4-inch piece pink handmade paper
- Matte spray sealer
- Low-tack masking tape
- Gem glue
- Black permanent marker

Instructions

1 Referring to photo throughout, assemble shelves according to manufacturer's instructions; slide drawers into place and lay unit on level surface, face up.

2 Lay stencil No. 1 across all drawer fronts, cascading from upper left to lower right. Secure stencil with low-tack tape.

3 Using sponge daubers, apply colors from both ink pads to open areas of stencil, alternating colors in a free-form fashion. Remove stencil; wipe excess ink off stencil. Let dry.

4 Spray stenciled chest and drawers with a light coat of matte sealer; let dry.

5 Align stencil No. 2 over inked area; tape in place. Repeat stenciling process using same colors. Remove stencil; wipe off excess ink. Let ink dry. Repeat step 4.

6 Squeeze dabs of adhesive onto centers of stenciled flowers.

Sprinkle small pinches of all colors of Rox onto wet glaze; let dry.

7 Move picture pebble around on printed origami paper to locate a soft, pastel floral area. Trace around pebble; cut out paper circle. Coat bottom of pebble with liquid adhesive; set atop paper circle. Repeat to apply paper circles to bottoms of all picture pebbles; let dry.

8 Glue pebbles to fronts of drawers to simulate drawer pulls.

9 Following Bejeweler's instructions, place one rhinestone in center of each pebble drawer pull.

10 Cut 2¼-inch square of pink handmade paper; round off corners. Referring to pattern, draw Japanese character for spring in center of pink paper square; fill in with black marker; let dry.

11 Sponge color from twilight ink pad onto paper around character; when dry, glue to chest as shown. ◆

When I began to stencil the front of this chest of drawers, I decided to stop after the second stencil because I liked the graphic, yet delicate, cherry blossom that had formed. I continued to build upon a calming Asian theme, adding just a touch of understated shimmer. I thought a chop mark would complete the composition, so I did some research, drew the Japanese character for "spring" and added it to one drawer.

—Mary Lynn Maloney

Gilded Stucco Treasure Box

Instead of using paint to stencil, add depth to your project by stenciling with a dimensional paste!

Design by Koren Russell

Materials
- 6½ x 8½-inch oval papier-mâché box with lid
- Pale green stucco
- Leaf scroll stencil
- Gold metallic stamp pad
- 15 jumbo (1¼-inch) flat glass marbles
- Palette knife
- Glass cement

"This was a leather-and-lace type of idea. A rough finish was needed to contrast with the smooth, flat marbles. The stucco texture provides the perfect companion since it offers texture along with color.

—Koren Russell

Instructions

1 Apply stucco to box with palette knife following manufacturer's instructions. Cover sides of box, applying only a very thin layer where lid overlaps box so lid will still fit. Cover top and sides of lid; let dry.

2 Cover box bottom with stucco; let dry.

3 Hold stencil in position over box with one hand. Spread stucco over stencil with other hand. Remove stencil; set aside to dry.

4 Continue stenciling to wrap design around box; set aside until all stucco is dry.

5 Lightly wipe stamp pad over raised areas of stencil and box.

6 Repeat step 5 to add more gold along stenciled design.

7 Glue three flat marbles into a stack, flat surface to rounded surface; repeat to create four more stacks of three flat marbles. Set aside to dry for 24 hours.

8 Glue marble stack flat side down to center of lid for handle; glue remaining stacks to bottom of box, flat sides to box, for feet. Let dry. ◆

Create
Vary the look of this box by using round balls for the feet and handle. Square blocks would also work well with a dark color and a geometric stencil to make a treasure box for your favorite man.

Gemstone Treasure Box

The Celtic feel of the stencil used in this design gives this box a masculine look.

Design by Mary Ayres

Materials
- 3½ x 3 x 6-inch wooden box with rounded top and hinged lid
- 7-inch motif stencil
- 8 bottle green glass pebbles
- 12 inches fine jute twine
- Acrylic craft paints: dark brown, dark green, off-white, metallic gold
- Medium green stamping ink pad
- Glass cement
- Paintbrushes: large round or square bristle, small and medium stencil brushes
- Masking tape
- Fine sandpaper
- Craft drill with small bit

Instructions

1 On front of box, drill a hole in center of lid edge and another ½ inch below it, in center of box front; holes should be just large enough to thread twine through them.

2 Paint exterior of box with two or three smooth coats dark brown, allowing paint to dry between coats; coverage should be opaque. Let dry.

3 Lightly sand surface and edges with sandpaper for "distressed" appearance. Dab ink pad onto surface, edges and corners of box; let dry.

4 Center stencil on top of box; secure with masking tape. Referring to directions for stenciling with a brush ("Painting Techniques," General Instructions, page 174), stencil entire design with gold, allowing brown to show through in places. Shade random areas of motif with dark green and off-white. Continue stencil over edges onto sides of lid and box if stencil is larger than top of box. Let dry.

5 Glue flat surfaces of pebbles symmetrically to stenciled design on top of box; let dry.

6 Thread jute through drilled holes; close box, then tie ends in a bow. Trim and fray ends. ◆

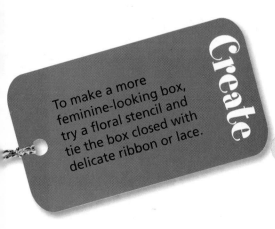

Create

To make a more feminine-looking box, try a floral stencil and tie the box closed with delicate ribbon or lace.

"*I like the way the large motif of this stencil wraps over the edges of the box. The shape of the box inspired the old sea trunk idea, and the mossy green makes it seem like the trunk has been submerged under water for a long time.*"

—**Mary Ayres**

Manhattan Desk Set

Textured handmade paper in deep
shades gives an uptown feel
to this set of desk accessories.

Designs by Judi Kauffman

HOUSE of WHITE BIRCHES
Berne, IN 46711
PUBLISHERS SINCE 1947

Materials
- Pair of hexagonal papier-mâché boxes—shorter one with lid, taller one with open top
- 2½ x 4¾ x 1-inch block of wood
- 6 round 1-inch red wooden beads
- Textured black mulberry paper
- Reptile-texture paper
- Square pattern stencil
- Crimson red ink pad
- Polished river stones
- Pencils or pens
- Craft drill with bits
- Craft glue

"This trio is masculine enough for a man's desk but equally appropriate for a woman with tailored tastes. I picture a sleek desk in a Manhattan penthouse, though my set will end up right here in a suburban rambler next to a bag of chocolates and a photo of my dog.
—Judi Kauffman"

Continued on page 107

Elegant Gem Torchère

Rich amber jewels give an exotic, tribal look to a plain floor lamp.

Design by June Fiechter

Materials
- Torchère-style lamp with removable plastic shade
- Black embossing stamp pad
- Black embossing enamel/powder
- Embossing heat tool
- Decoupage glue/sealer
- Desired stencil
- Brown paper lunch bag
- Stamp pads: deep green, brown
- Assorted glass gems

Instructions

1 Tear paper bag into pieces. Use decoupage glue/sealer to glue pieces to inner and outer surfaces of lamp shade; let dry.

2 Position stencil over outer surface of lamp shade as desired and stamp with black embossing pad.

Sprinkle embossing powder over wet ink; heat with embossing tool. Repeat to cover exterior of lamp shade as desired.

3 Press deep green and brown stamp pads over interior and exterior of lamp shade, wiping off excess ink with a paper towel as you go. Let dry.

4 Glue gems around rim of lamp shade; let dry. ◆

" This lamp was very inexpensive, but the plastic shade wasn't impressive! Simply gluing on paper was a great start but the stamped stencil finished it nicely. I opted to use embossing enamel over embossing ink, which, when heat-set, was a good surface on which to rub other colors of ink. I chose thin gems to add a touch of class. "

—June Fiechter

Change the paper, stencil and color of the jewels to match your own style of decorating.

Create

Gold-Studded Frame

Less is more in this simple project. Gold studs on glass accent the easy stenciling of the mat.

Design by Sharon M. Reinhart

Materials
- 5 x 7-inch glass frame
- 5 x 7-inch tan photo mat
- Green-brown permanent ink stamp suitable for glass
- Metallic gold round cabochons: 2 medium, 4 small
- 3¾ x 1-inch horizontal stencil motifs to fit across top and bottom of photo mat
- Stencil sponge dauber
- Gold leafing pen
- Clear-drying jewel glue
- Alcohol swab
- 5 x 7-inch piece card stock
- Painter's tape
- Toothpick
- Lint-free cloth

> *The idea for this project began with a glass frame, which is a quick, inexpensive way to display your photos. The simple stencil design was the inspiration for the jewels and photos with which the frame is partnered.*
> —Sharon M. Reinhart

Instructions

1 Remove clips and backing from frame. Wipe glass with alcohol swab; dry with lint-free cloth.

2 Using ruler and pencil, mark horizontal and vertical center lines on card stock; this piece will be helpful for centering stencil.

3 Place card-stock template under glass; secure to work surface at two corners with painter's tape. Center and secure stencil on top of glass.

4 Using sponge dauber and a gentle pouncing motion, apply ink in open areas of stencil. Let dry, then remove stencil. Clean stencil immediately with rubbing alcohol.

5 Referring to photo throughout, glue cabochons to opposite (unstenciled) side of glass to accent stenciled designs, applying drops of glue to backs of cabochons with toothpick. Let dry.

6 Color fronts of frame clips with gold leafing pen; let dry.

7 Affix photo to mat with tape. Place backing piece down, followed by photo mat and finally glass, stenciled side down. Following manufacturer's instructions, attach clips so that gold sides face out. ◆

Create

Make this project as simple or complex as you wish by varying the stencil and adding more studs as embellishment.

Harlequin Photo Tray

Frame your favorite face in the center of this functional tray!

Design by Katie Hacker

Materials
- Wooden tray
- Stencils: harlequin pattern, scroll background, "smile," "joy," "love," "wish"
- Royal blue pigment ink pad
- 4mm silver acrylic rhinestones
- White acrylic craft paint
- 1-inch foam paintbrush
- White card stock
- Clear embossing powder
- Embossing heat gun
- Satin-finish acrylic sealer
- Craft glue
- Gem glue
- Adhesive tape *or* painter's tape
- Scrap paper
- Glass or Plexiglas, cut to fit inside tray (optional)

Instructions

1 Paint tray with light coat of white paint; let dry.

2 Referring to photo throughout, center harlequin stencil on tray; tape in place. Tap ink pad over stencil; let dry.

3 Rub ink pad lightly over top edges of sides of tray; sprinkle embossing powder over wet color. Using heat gun, emboss powder and heat-set ink.

4 Paint unstenciled areas of tray with sealer; let dry.

5 Cut two 9¾ x ⅜-inch strips card stock. Lay them on scrap paper and rub ink pad back and forth over strips; let dry.

6 Cut two 9¾ x 1½-inch strips card stock. Lay them on scrap paper, position scroll stencil on top and tape in place. Tap ink pad over stencil; let dry.

7 Cut a piece of card stock ¾ inch larger all around than photo. Position one word stencil in center of each side of card-stock mat. Tap ink pad over stencil; let dry. Rub ink pad lightly over spaces between words; let dry. Glue photo in center of card stock.

I like the fresh, clean combination of blue and white. For this project, I decided to highlight a favorite photo on an item that could be merely decorative or actually put to good use. Pigment ink stamp pads lend a brushed, airy quality to the stenciled areas and the rhinestones contribute a playful touch.

—Katie Hacker

8 Glue card stock with photo over harlequin design in center of tray. Glue stenciled scroll strips into tray along side edges; glue a blue strip along edge of each scroll strip.

9 Glue rhinestones to top edges of tray handles.

Note: *If you plan to use tray, cover inside with glass or Plexiglas to prevent damage to the design.* ◆

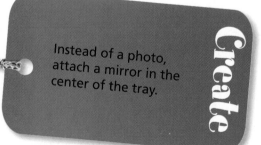

Create

Instead of a photo, attach a mirror in the center of the tray.

Victorian Beaded Lamp Shade

Several shades of paint add depth to the stencil work on this shade. Jewels add sparkle.

Design by Sherian Frey

Materials
- Lamp with smooth shade
- Vine border stencil
- Multicolored ink pad with yellow and green
- Stenciling brushes
- Amber faceted gems in assorted sizes
- Coordinating beaded fringe
- Coordinating braid, cord or gimp trim
- Craft glue
- Clips *or* spring-type clothespins
- Transparent tape (optional)

Delicate colors, flowing designs, sparkling gems and beads are all things that remind me of genteel, feminine style. I found that using a stamp ink pad for color ensures light color application to the stencil brush and results in a delicately painted stencil. Subtle color variations add to the elegance of this lamp.

—Sherian Frey

Create

Purchase a lamp shade with beads already attached, or add beaded trim to a recycled shade.

Project Note
It is recommended that you practice stenciling on paper before working on the lamp shade. Referring to directions for stenciling with a brush ("Painting Techniques," General Instructions, page 174), apply ink from stamp pads with stencil brushes. Apply lightest color first, then go back over selected areas with darker color. Stabilize the stencil with tape or clips before applying colors. In some areas, you may need to further secure the stencil by holding it in place with your fingers.

Instructions

1 Plan stencil placement for best flow of design around shade. Clip stencil securely in place.

2 Add color in segments large enough to make pattern but small enough to clip stencil flat against shade, moving stencil and clips as necessary. Let dry.

3 Referring to photo throughout, glue gems in place on shade. Glue bead trim around bottom edge of shade and coordinating braid trim around top of shade. ***Note:*** *Neutral trim may be brushed with ink from pads to match border of beaded fringe.* ◆

Perky Daisy Tissue Box Cover

Silk flower accents pop out of the stenciled frames on the sides of this tissue box cover. A perky bow adds whimsy.

Design by Lisa Galvin

Materials

- Unfinished wooden tissue box cover for boutique-style tissues
- Kiwi green satin-finish spray paint
- Funky leaf and fun flower stencil
- Pigment ink pads: dark green, burgundy, gold
- Ultrafine clear embossing powder
- Embossing heat gun
- 4 (3½- to 4-inch) off-white/cream silk daisies
- Kiwi green wire-edge ⅝-inch satin ribbon
- 4 small flat-back glass pebbles
- Ultrafine sandpaper
- Tack cloth
- Masking tape
- Hot-glue gun

Instructions

1 Sand box cover; wipe off dust with tack cloth. Spray box cover with several light coats of kiwi green, letting paint dry between coats and after last application.

2 Working on one side of box at a time and referring to photo throughout, secure stencils with masking tape, positioning a rectangle of tiny squares in center, a vertical bar on left and right sides of squares rectangle, and an outer rectangle of tiny leaves around bars and squares as shown. Mask off areas as needed to keep stray colors from corrupting them.

3 Using ink pads, apply burgundy to squares, gold to vertical bars and dark green to leaves. Following manufacturer's instructions, apply clear embossing powder to stenciled areas; tap off excess. Complete embossing with heat gun, holding it at least 6 inches from surface to keep paint from bubbling.

4 Remove stems, plastic backing and centers from silk daisies. Hot-glue a flower in center of each stenciled frame as shown. Hot-glue pebble in center of each flower.

5 Wrap kiwi green wire-edge ribbon around top; tie in bow at front corner. ◆

Adding a charming effect to any room, this simple box is not only easy to create—it's useful, too! Combine glass gems with ribbon, silk flowers and your favorite color tones and you can easily create a whole set of home decor accessories to coordinate with this project!
—Lisa Galvin

Romantic Rose Candle

Change the look of a purchased candle by covering it in a stenciled tissue-paper wrap. Studs add a bit of shine.

Design by Lorine Mason

Materials
- Candle
- Stencils: rose, scroll
- Pigment ink stamp pads: red, orange, yellow, light green
- Clear embossing powder
- ¼-inch silver metal studs
- White tissue paper
- Embossing heat tool

Project Note
Candle is for decorative purposes only and should not be burned.

Instructions

1 Measure candle's height and circumference with tape measure; cut tissue paper to this measurement. Center rose stencil on tissue.

2 Apply color to open areas of stencil by tapping with ink pads, beginning with lighter shades in center and progressing to darker shades on outer edges of leaves and petals.

3 Cut a piece of tissue paper large enough to cover the stenciled rose; lay tissue gently over rose design so as not to smear it. Continue to stencil remaining tissue paper around rose using scroll stencil and light green stamp pad.

4 Lay stenciled tissue on top of a large piece of plain tissue and sprinkle entire stenciled piece with embossing powder. Tap off excess and return unused powder to

container. Emboss stenciled paper with heating tool.

5 Center embossed stenciled design on front of candle. While carefully holding tissue in place, use heating tool to heat candle slowly, allowing heated wax to melt into tissue design. Take care to keep heat tool moving; you want only to melt and liquefy the top layer of wax so that it saturates tissue. If you hold the heat tool in one spot too long, you will melt too much of the candle, leaving flat spots. Work your way around the candle, smoothing the design around

the top and bottom edges, until a thin layer of wax covers the design; let cool.

6 Press silver studs into candle, highlighting the stenciled design. ◆

Create

Virtually any look can be created by varying the stencil and candle color.

Candles are a fairly inexpensive way to set a mood in your home. Why not dress up a plain candle with a favorite flower? Roses add a bit of romance to the candlelight.

—Lorine Mason

Trailing Vine Steppingstone

A background stencil makes it easy to create a delicate floral scene.

Design by Samantha McNesby

Materials

- Dark green permanent ink stamp pad
- 32 clear round faceted acrylic crystal rhinestones
- Allover botanical-design stencil
- Acrylic paints: ivory, metallic gold
- 12-inch square concrete steppingstone
- Cotton-tip swabs *or* rubber-tipped paintbrush
- 1-inch foam brush
- ¼-inch flat paintbrush
- Spray adhesive (optional)
- Permanent glue for nonporous surfaces
- Satin-finish spray sealer

Instructions

1 Using foam brush, base-coat steppingstone with two coats ivory paint, letting paint dry completely between coats and after last application.

I like doing projects to use outdoors, but it is difficult to find products that will stand up to the elements. Permanent dye pads stand up well to weather. Using a foam brush and cotton-tip swabs to apply the ink let me complete the stencil quickly, with little mess. I love the addition of gold and gemstones; I don't think a project is really complete until you add a bit of sparkle!

—**Samantha McNesby**

2 Spray back of stencil with adhesive if desired. Position stencil right side up on steppingstone.

3 Using swabs or rubber-tipped brush, apply ink from stamp pad to stone inside openings in stencil. Work on a small area at a time and reposition stencil as needed until entire top surface is covered. Let dry.

4 Rub surface of ink pad along sides of steppingstone to ink

entire surface; let dry. *Tip: Lay steppingstone across top of bowl or box and rotate bowl as needed.*

5 Using ¼-inch brush and metallic gold paint, apply gold border around top of steppingstone; let dry.

6 Spray stone with satin-finish sealer; let dry.

7 Glue acrylic crystal rhinestones around edge of steppingstone, on top of gold border. Let dry completely. ◆

Create Choose another background stencil that matches the theme of your garden. How about jumping frogs for a pond, or dragonflies and ladybugs for a flower garden?

Manhattan Desk Set

Continued from page 99

Instructions

1 Referring to photo throughout, drill five ½-inch-deep holes in wooden block large enough to hold pencils or pens.

2 Cover box lid, interior and exterior of open box and all surfaces of wooden block with black mulberry paper. While covering wooden block, poke tip of pencil or point of small scissors through paper to keep holes for pencils open.

3 Using ink pad, randomly stencil bottom of box with squares. Let dry.

4 Glue red wooden beads to bottom corners of box for feet.

5 Cut strips of reptile-texture paper and glue as shown to wood block, box lid, and front and sides of tall container. Lay tall container flat on work surface, front side up. Glue polished river stones between pencil

Create Changing the colors from darks to pastels immediately changes the look and feel of this set.

holes, to lid of box, and to front of tall container as shown. Make sure glue is completely dry before setting tall container upright. ◆

Midnight Glitz Evening Bag

A few sparkling rhinestones and some simple stenciling are all you need to add glamour to a basic black bag.

Design by Mary Lynn Maloney

This black satin bag is a perfect accessory for that little black dress. Just a touch of moonlight, silver and sparkly rhinestones give the bag a classy touch.

—Mary Lynn Maloney

Materials

- 6¼ x 6½-inch black satin purse
- Scrolling vine stencil
- Frost white fabric stamping ink pad
- Small pouncing sponge
- Pearl blue pearlescent fabric paint
- Small liner paintbrush
- Austrian crystal heat-set rhinestones: 8 (⅛-inch) fuchsia, 7 (¼-inch) jet black–blue, 3 (⅛-inch) sky blue
- Large-hole beads: 2 fuchsia, 1 blue
- 6-inch square heavy cardboard
- Rhinestone setting tool
- Hair dryer

Instructions

1 Slip heavy cardboard into purse. Referring to photo throughout, lay stencil on top of purse where desired. Tap pouncing sponge onto white ink pad; tap off excess ink onto scrap paper. Using a straight up-and-down motion and then a swirling motion, sponge ink into open areas of stencil.

Carefully lift stencil and clean it with a paper towel. Replace stencil in another area of purse and repeat stenciling as desired; remove and clean stencil.

2 Using liner and pearl blue paint, add thin highlight lines along edges on one side of stenciled scrolls and leaves. Heat-set paints with hair dryer for 45 seconds; do not hold dryer too close to purse.

3 Heat up rhinestone setting tool. Follow manufacturer's instructions for picking up and placing rhinestones. Position black rhinestones at intersections of stenciled leaves; add fuchsia rhinestone next to each black one; alternate fuchsia, blue and black rhinestones along bottom edge of purse.

4 Cut top of purse handle in two. Thread fuchsia bead onto each half; push down toward base of handle. Hold cut ends together; thread

through blue bead. Knot handle ends together; push blue bead close to knot. ◆

Fun & Funky Purse

Paint, jewels and simple embroidery stitches combine to create a girl-power purse.

Design by Chris Malone

Materials
- 6 x 9-inch natural canvas purse with flap closure and shoulder strap
- Rainbow dye ink pad
- Stencils: heart and flower, large spirals
- 6-strand embroidery floss: black, light green, dark green
- Rhinestones: 5 (7mm) green, 2 (11mm) yellow, 1 (11mm) pink
- 60 inches green chenille cord
- 12 assorted plastic beads with large holes
- Eye-shadow applicators *or* cotton swabs
- Embroidery needle
- Fabric adhesive
- Scrap cardboard
- Masking tape

Instructions

1 Referring to photo throughout, position flower, heart and swirl stencils on purse and flap; hold in place with masking tape.

2 Stencil designs by dabbing eye-shadow applicator onto ink pad and rubbing color onto fabric inside stencil openings. Sample has pink heart, blue flower and three dark green spirals on purse and lavender flower with two light green spirals on flap. Motifs should be darker around edges and lightly colored in center. Let dry.

3 Place a scrap of cardboard inside purse before adding embroidery to keep needle from piercing back of purse. Using 2 strands black floss, sew running stitch around heart and flowers near motifs' outer edges. Sew chain stitch over spirals, using 2 strands dark green on spirals on purse and 2 strands lighter green for spirals on flap.

4 Glue green rhinestones at ends of spirals; glue yellow rhinestones in centers of flowers and pink rhinestone to heart.

5 Untie knot of shoulder strap on right side of purse. Insert one end of chenille trim and retie knot with trim inside, leaving 6-inch tail below knot. Wrap trim around strap along its length in a loose spiral. Untie knot on opposite side and re-knot, capturing end of trim as before, leaving an 8-inch tail; trim as needed.

6 Slip five beads onto shorter chenille end, covering end of trim with tape if needed to thread beads on easily. Knot end of trim to hold beads in place. In same fashion, thread seven beads on other end of chenille trim. ◆

It's always fun to experiment with products in a new way or on a new surface. I was surprised at how easy and effective it is to stencil with stamping inks onto fabric. Foam eye-shadow applicators purchased at a discount store are perfect for applying the ink. My granddaughter loved this project, so we found another purse for her and discovered that stenciling with stamping ink is a great project for kids.

—Chris Malone

Sparkly Summer Tote

Carry your summer necessities in style in a canvas tote accented with background stencils and assorted jewels. A sequined appliqué adds a fun touch of sparkle.

Design by Vicki Schreiner

Materials

- Large pocket tote
- Background stencils: leaves, swirls
- Magnolia stencil
- Fabric ink pads: ash rose, burgundy, celery green, chocolate, dark green, lavender
- Assorted faceted rhinestones *or* gemstones (sample uses ⅛-inch to 9/16-inch rhinestones in shades of pink, light green and lavender to complement paints and sequined butterfly)
- Fabric adhesive
- 20 inches ⅜-inch decorative trim
- Sequined butterfly patch
- Pencil with unused eraser
- Masking tape
- Cosmetic sponge wedges
- Toothpicks

Instructions

1 Wash and dry tote without fabric softener according to manufacturer's instructions; iron as needed.

2 *Use applicator sponges to apply ink for stenciling:* Dab fat end of sponge on ink pad, then dab onto project, reloading sponge as needed. For shading, apply additional ink in a second color on top of first; let dry. **Note:** *To conserve sponges, when you complete one color, cut off inked end with scissors, leaving fresh sponge for applying the next color.* Use paper towels to protect any areas of bag where you do not want to apply color.

Stencil bag as follows:

Top section: Referring to photo throughout, apply swirls background stencil with ash rose, moving stencil across bag as needed. Tap flat, round end of unused pencil eraser in ink pad and apply scattered dots of lavender between swirls.

Middle section: Center magnolia stencil on center panel. Mask off all other areas of stencil with masking tape. Stencil leaves with celery green; shade with dark green. Stencil stems with chocolate. Stencil flowers with ash rose; shade with burgundy. Stencil flower center with chocolate.

Bottom section: Apply leaves background stencil with celery green, moving stencil across bag as needed. Use bullet-point coloring tool as a paintbrush to apply light amounts of ash rose shading to each leaf.

3 Use fabric adhesive to attach trim across top of pockets about ½ inch below edge; glue rhinestones to trim and bag as desired. Glue sequined butterfly to bottom right corner of tote. ◆

Create

If you don't have faceted rhinestones on hand, substitute circles and dots of ultrafine glitter in coordinating colors. Most are washable—but check the package before applying to bag.

My inspiration here was simply the tote. What better way to express your personal style than to carry an embellished tote bag? You can never have enough totes in all kinds of shapes and sizes to carry every little "this and that."

—Vicki Schreiner

WINDOW-CLING PAINT
Fabric

Window-cling paint isn't just for windows! Our designers have combined it with fabric and other crafting materials to make unique jewelry and  home accents you're sure to love. Substitute your favorite fabrics and colors to make these projects uniquely your own!

Craft Closet Challenge
Antique Planter

The challenge—each designer needs to create a project using the materials we selected (and one or two more items they add).

Design by June Fiechter

"In this project, the look of solder holds together aged painted ceramic mixed with stone pottery. I've never been one to appreciate fancy, ornate planters because I think they detract from the plants inside. So I chose to downplay this piece and create an antique-looking planter like ones that might have been stored in my grandmother's potting shed."

—June Fiechter

Materials

- Timeless Accents Large (11-inch) Ball Pot from FloraCraft
- Strip of scrap fabric long enough to reach around pot
- Paint Jewels window-cling paints from Delta: jade green, golden topaz, garnet red, black onyx
- Paint Jewels Liquid Lead from Delta: white, pewter
- Easy Metal silver leafing *and* leafing adhesive from Amaco
- Aleene's Faux Easy Antique Fragile Crackle Kit from Duncan
- Fabric adhesive
- Assorted foam brushes
- Filbert paintbrush
- Matte spray varnish

Instructions

1 Referring to photo throughout, cut fabric 2 inches wide and long enough to go around widest part of pot; glue in place.

2 Mix equal parts jade green, golden topaz and garnet red paints. Using a foam brush and a daubing motion, sponge one coat of mixture onto pot, avoiding fabric strip. Let dry.

3 Sponge a coat of black onyx paint over first coat; let dry.

4 Sponge all painted surfaces with a light coat of pewter liquid leading; let dry.

5 Referring to manufacturer's instructions, use filbert brush to apply a heavy coat of step 1 mixture from the crackle kit over the fabric. Keep the surface on which you are working horizontal as you go around the pot, and avoid touching the wet crackle.

6 Apply step 2 liquid over step 1 as directed.

7 When crackled surface is completely dry, brush on brown translucent glaze from crackle kit. Work on a small area at a time and use paper towel to wipe off excess glaze immediately. Let dry completely.

8 Squeeze a line of white liquid leading along both edges of fabric strip.

9 Apply leafing adhesive along edges of fabric; let dry.

10 Apply silver leafing to adhesive according to manufacturer's instructions; wipe off excess with brush.

11 Spray entire project with matte-finish varnish; let dry. ◆

Craft Closet Challenge

It's a Pot—It's a Table

Design by Judi Kauffman

If I even look at a plant it wilts. Since this chapter challenge included a large pot, I thought I'd better make it into something other than a container for something green. The shape and size looked like Asian porcelain pieces that are so popular for table bases, so I decided to make one. I chose colors that will look good in my home, but it's easy to customize the project. Pick any patterned mulberry paper and paint colors that go with your decor. I used a 16-inch tabletop so that the table will fit in a small space, but the pot would look fine with any size up to 30 inches. For a bigger table, start with a larger pot and plant stand.

—Judi Kauffman

Materials

- Timeless Accents Large (11-inch) Ball Pot from FloraCraft
- Paint Jewels window-cling paints from Delta: turquoise, golden topaz, ruby red, smoky brown
- Wooden 7¾-inch-diameter plant stand
- 16-inch round wooden table top
- Ivory acrylic paint (optional)
- 9 (12-inch squares) patterned mulberry paper
- Scraps of 4 assorted fabrics to coordinate with mulberry paper
- Acrylic adhesive medium
- 4 cosmetic sponge wedges
- Old paintbrush
- Acrylic sealer (optional)

Instructions

1 Tear patterned paper into random pieces. Referring to photo throughout, use paintbrush to apply adhesive to pot and paper, one piece at a time, and apply paper to pot to create a collage, leaving space between pieces. Let glue dry.

2 Using a different cosmetic wedge for each color, dab paints randomly between and onto paper pieces, giving a mottled effect; let dry.

3 Base-coat table top with ivory paint if wood is not finished; let dry.

4 Tear patterned paper into random pieces. Use paintbrush to apply adhesive to tabletop and paper, one piece at a time, and apply paper to cover entire surface. Let glue dry, then turn tabletop over and repeat to cover bottom surface; let dry.

5 Tear fabrics into 1-inch strips; pull threads to fray edges. Tear one strip into 1-inch pieces and pull threads to create small squares.

6 Arrange fabric strips and squares on tabletop as desired. Apply adhesive to fabric with paintbrush and add them to tabletop, brushing frayed edges outward so that they look like fringe.

7 Randomly sponge turquoise paint onto tabletop to add extra shine and color that matches collage on pot. Let dry.

8 Set pot on plant stand; center tabletop on pot.

9 Coat tabletop with acrylic sealer if desired, or top with a glass bevel-edge table topper. ◆

Craft Closet Challenge
Fabric & Fibers Planter

Design by Mary Lynn Maloney

Materials
- Timeless Accents Large (11-inch) Ball Pot from FloraCraft
- Paint Jewels window-cling paints from Delta: citrine yellow, turquoise, teal quartz, sapphire, white pearl
- 8½ x 11-inch piece heavy white card stock
- Marbling comb
- 18 x 22-inch piece red/multi floral fabric
- 1 yard 1½-inch-wide mustard yellow ribbon
- Decorative fibers in primary colors
- Fabric adhesive
- Jewel cement
- Superglue
- Iron

Instructions

1 Mark 8-inch square on card stock with pencil. Following color order as presented in Materials list, squeeze out lines of each paint onto card stock, butting colors against each other (its OK if they run together). Fill entire square, repeating colors in order as needed. Run marbling comb though wet paint, creating a pleasing pattern. Let dry for several hours.

2 Cut three 7 x 18-inch strips of fabric; turn under all long edges ⅜ inch and press. Glue down long edges with fabric glue. Overlap short ends of strips ¼ inch and glue together to create one long strip.

3 Cut dried marbled painted square into 1 x 4-inch strips. Choose your five favorites, holding the rest in reserve.

4 Cut five 4-inch pieces of mustard yellow ribbon. Lay one marbled paint strip along center of one ribbon strip; secure with fabric adhesive. Repeat with remaining ribbon and marbled pieces; let dry.

5 Gather long fabric strip at one glued-together short edge; wrap with one of the marbled paint/ribbon pieces, forming a ring around the fabric. Glue ends of ring together in back with jewel cement. Dab a bit of cement under front of ring between it and fabric. Repeat around ring at even intervals; let cement dry.

6 Beginning with center ring, use superglue to adhere ring to rim of pot. Repeat at each ring section, allowing fabric to fall in swag between rings. Trim excess fabric as needed and join ends of fabric strip so that entire pot rim is covered.

7 Glue red long-fringed fiber around top lid of pot; repeat.

> I wanted to keep this planter rather simple because I think the shape itself is quite pleasing to the eye. I decided that all it needed was a little soft, fuzzy texture at the rim to contrast with the smooth surface of the sides.
> —Mary Lynn Maloney

8 Cut fuzzy multicolored fiber into 10 (16-inch) pieces. Gather two together and loop around swagged fabric between two of the rings on pot rim. Pull softly to gather and tighten. Add a dab of fabric glue between pot and back of fiber loop. Tie a knot about ¾ inch from bottom of hanging fibers.

9 Cut reserved marbled paint strips into 10 (¾-inch) squares. Sandwich ends of one hanging fuzzy-fiber loop just above knot between two squares; secure with jewel cement. ◆

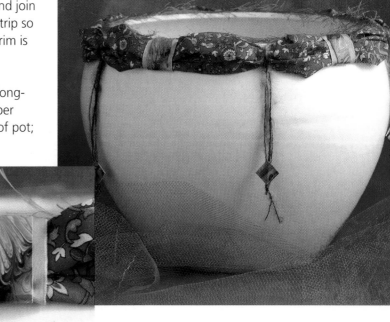

Stained Glass Toile Suncatcher

Showcase a favorite floral motif with a faux stained-glass frame.

Design by Mary Ayres

Materials
- 4 x 6-inch vertical oval blank hanging glass panel
- 4 (7/16-inch) flat white pearl buttons
- Blue toile fabric
- Window-cling paints: light blue, primary blue
- Pewter liquid leading
- Craft knife
- Tracing paper
- Thick white craft glue

Instructions

1 Place glass on tracing paper; trace around edge with pencil. Remove glass; draw an oval border ⅝ inch inside traced line.

2 Carefully cut out paper oval. Fold in half vertically, then horizontally, then in quarters and then in eighths (you will have a narrow "pie wedge"). Unfold paper and using pencil, mark all fold lines within the ⅝-inch border so that border is made up of equally spaced and symmetrical sections.

3 Place paper pattern under glass. Trace over lines with pewter leading following manufacturer's instructions, keeping tip of tube slightly above glass and allowing paint to flow from tube. Let leading dry 1–2 hours. (When dry, scrape or cut any excess leading off glass.)

4 Following manufacturer's instructions, outline and fill in shapes in border, alternating with light blue and primary blue. Let dry until colors are completely transparent. (Painted side is front of suncatcher.)

5 Place glass on top of fabric, painted side up, and centering a pleasing design inside frame. Trace around glass with pencil. Cut out fabric just inside line.

6 Place fabric on back of glass; trim any fabric edges that extend

I have a collection of old buttons and I try to use them in craft projects whenever I can. While the beautiful toile fabric inspired this design, I couldn't resist adding old pearl buttons.

—Mary Ayres

beyond glass. Run a bead of glue around edge of fabric on front; press fabric onto back of glass.

7 Glue pearl buttons to front of glass as shown; let dry before hanging. ◆

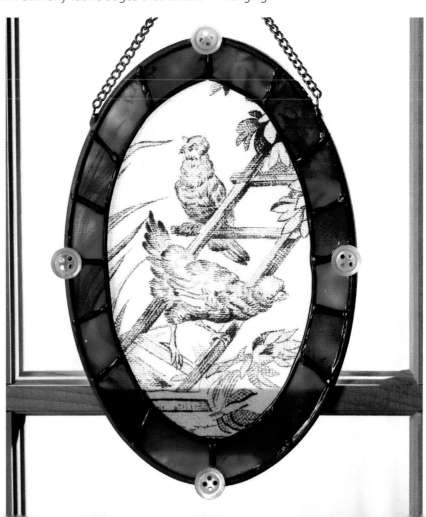

Stained Glass Butterfly Box

Glass paint on wood creates a stained glass look without using a glass cutter!

Design by Sherian Frey

Materials

- 8¼ x 3¼ x 5⅜-inch wooden box with lid
- Window-cling paints: garnet red, berry red, amethyst, sapphire
- Gold liquid leading
- Wood stain *or* acrylic paint
- Small flat paintbrush
- Gloss-finish sealer
- Fabric
- Spray adhesive
- Craft glue
- Transfer paper
- Poster board *or* cardboard cut from cereal box
- Transparent tape

Create Choose a different motif for the box lid. How about a dragonfly or a ladybug? Children's coloring books are good sources of line drawings; simply enlarge the chosen motif to fit on a copy machine.

Instructions

1 Tape transfer paper and butterfly pattern to top of box. Trace over pattern lines to transfer butterfly to box lid. In same fashion, transfer pattern for box sides to front, back and ends of box.

2 Lay box so that back is facing up. Referring to manufacturer's instructions, apply liquid leading directly from bottle along pattern lines. **Note:** *If needed, practice making straight lines and curlicues with leading on scrap paper first.* Allow leaded surface to lie flat until dry.

3 Referring to photo and manufacturer's instructions throughout, apply colors directly from bottle to sections of leaded design. Fill small areas by dripping paint from toothpick. Pop bubbles with toothpick. Allow painted surface to lie flat until dry.

4 Repeat steps 2 and 3 to lead and paint ends of box, then front, and finally, butterfly on top of box.

5 After painting is complete and dry, stain or paint remaining exposed wood. Let dry, then apply sealer; let dry.

6 Referring to diagram for box liner, cut shape from poster board, choosing correct cutting lines for top or bottom of box. Score along dotted lines; hold ruler along scored lines and fold up tabs at sides and ends. Test fit inside box; trim and/or adjust as needed.

7 Spray cardboard liner with adhesive. Lay facedown on wrong side of fabric. Trim fabric in corner at 45-degree angles; along straight edges, trim fabric to leave ¼ inch extra all around. Fold excess fabric smoothly over edges to back of cardboard; secure with craft glue. Glue completed liner inside box.

8 Repeat steps 6 and 7 to line other half of box. ◆

I enjoy working with fabric, I like boxes and containers, and I enjoy working with the various paints that produce stained glass effects on different surfaces. Designing this unique project provided the opportunity and challenge to use all three and decorate a box both inside and out.

—Sherian Frey

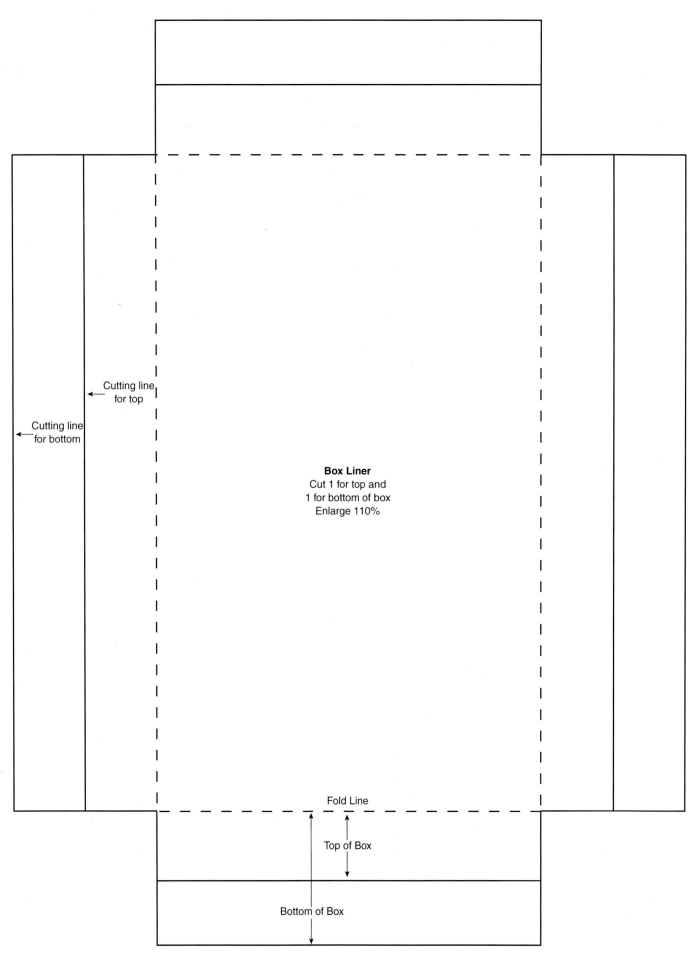

Cutting line for top

Cutting line for bottom

Box Liner
Cut 1 for top and
1 for bottom of box
Enlarge 110%

Fold Line

Top of Box

Bottom of Box

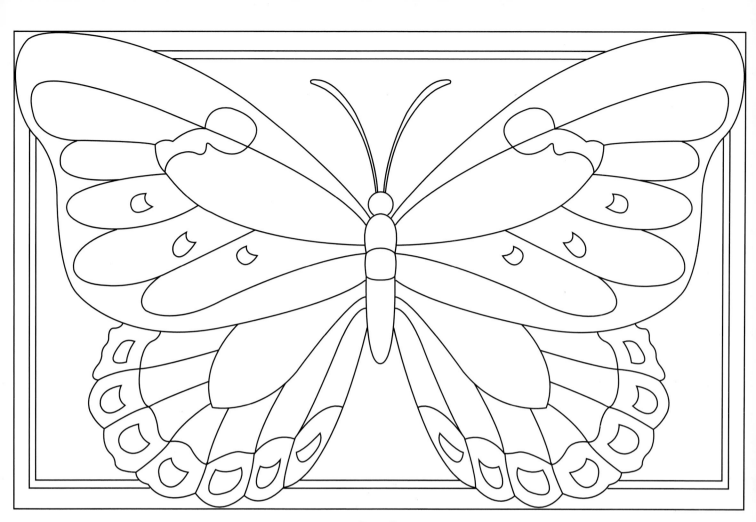

Butterfly

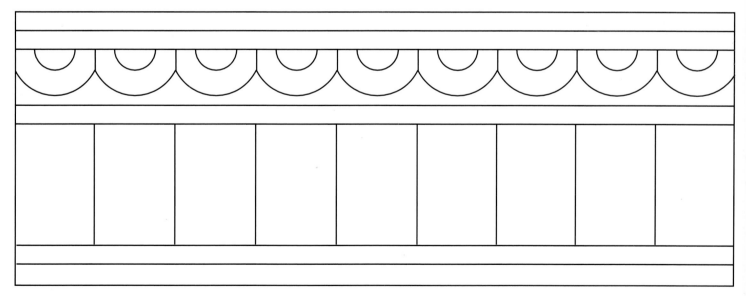

Box Sides

Garden Window

Bring the outdoors inside and enjoy summer year-round with this nature-inspired window art.

Design by Lisa Galvin

Materials
- 20 x 25-inch paned window
- Oak gel stain
- White acrylic paint
- Matte-finish acrylic spray sealer
- Crackle medium
- Pewter liquid leading
- Window-cling paints: amber, ivory, crystal clear, kelly green, ruby red
- Large and small glass pebbles
- Clear seed beads
- 2 wrought-iron dragonfly drawer pulls
- Wrought-iron twig-shaped drawer pull
- Small flat paintbrush
- 2 (1¼-inch) screw eyes
- 2 (1-inch) open S-hooks
- 25 inches #1/0 brass safety chain
- 3 x 40-inch strip coordinating fabric
- Coordinating silk butterfly
- Coordinating thread
- Craft drill with bits
- 1½-inch paintbrush
- Window cleaner
- Hot-glue gun
- Fine-grit sandpaper
- Tack cloth
- Scrap paper
- Masking tape
- Craft stick
- Razor blade
- Wood filler
- Sewing machine (optional)

Instructions

1 Referring to photo throughout, drill holes for attaching handle and knobs. **Note:** As windows are typically thicker than most drawer fronts, it may be necessary to purchase longer screws or use a slightly larger drill bit and countersink holes from the back of the frame, drilling only about ⅜ inch deep. Switch to a smaller drill bit sized to fit screws on handle and knobs, and drill hole all the way through in center of previously drilled hole. Fill any gouges or imperfections with wood filler; let dry. Sand lightly to smooth surface and remove rough edges. Wipe with tack cloth.

2 Clean window with window cleaner and paper towels. Cover glass panes with scrap paper held in place with masking tape.

3 Working on one side of frame at a time, apply gel stain; let dry. Brush on crackle medium. Following manufacturer's directions, apply top coat of white acrylic paint; paint will begin to crackle immediately and continue until dry. Let dry.

4 Spray dry frame with acrylic sealer. Let dry. Use straight edge of razor to remove excess paint from glass.

5 Attach screw eyes in top of frame.

6 Make several long, straight lines of liquid leading onto a spare pane of glass (or onto a pane removed from window frame). Let dry for 36–48 hours, until completely dry.

7 Photocopy patterns of leaf and tulip several times in several sizes for a more realistic look. (Bend tips of some leaves as shown.)

8 Referring to photo throughout, secure patterns on wrong side of window glass with masking tape.

9 Peel leading from glass (step 6) and apply to right side of window glass along pattern lines. Apply lines to bottom to simulate ground. Conceal joints with drops of liquid leading; let dry completely.

10 Hot-glue glass pebbles to glass as shown.

11 To create "ground," place a few dots of kelly green and ivory on one section; apply amber, swirling it into green and ivory paints to mix. Apply seed beads and press into window color. Repeat in remaining sections until ground is finished.

An avid gardener, I have a passion for flowers. Created in "shabby chic" style, this window will always make me think of my favorite time of year—spring!

—Lisa Galvin

Create

Recycle old windows in different shapes and sizes. The motifs used in this project will adapt easily to other windows.

12 Apply colors in remaining sections as shown, using a swirling motion and working color to outer edges; add just a sprinkling of seed beads in various spots for additional glimmer. Swirl ivory with ruby and/or green paints for desired effects. Let window lay flat until paint is completely dry.

13 Hot-glue butterfly to window as shown.

14 *Hanger:* Turn under 3-inch ends of fabric strip ¼ inch; stitch by hand or machine. Fold strip in half lengthwise, right sides facing, and stitch ¼ inch from raw edges to create casing; turn fabric tube right side out and slip over chain. Attach chain to screw eyes with S-hooks, using pliers to close ends of hooks. Adjust fabric fullness along chain.

15 Attach knobs and handle. ◆

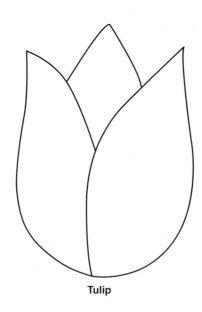

Tulip

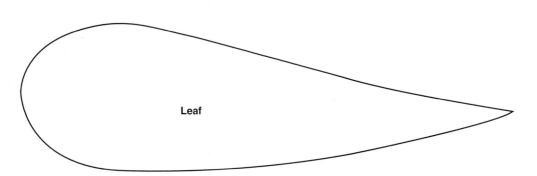

Leaf

Gypsy Vase

Purchased beaded trim adds an easy embellishment to a fabric-draped vase. Dripped-on glass paint creates the look of hand-blown glass.

Design by Mary Lynn Maloney

Materials
- 7½ x 3½-inch glass vase with narrow neck
- Window-cling transparent paints: yellow, burgundy, orange
- 8 x 10-inch sheet styrene
- Tall can of spray paint *or* can of similar size
- 18 x 22-inch piece turquoise gauzy, chiffon-type fabric
- ½ yard amber/bronze beaded fringe
- Fabric glue

Instructions

1 Clean vase with soap and water; dry thoroughly. Place styrene sheet on level work surface; set can of spray paint in center of styrene sheet. Turn vase upside down and set over can of spray paint to suspend vase without letting it touch the styrene sheet.

2 Squeeze yellow paint down sides of vase, letting it run down and turning styrene sheet to turn vase. While still wet, add orange and burgundy paints, squeezing them onto the sides of the vase so that they run down and run together. Continue until vase is covered.

3 Let vase dry undisturbed for 12–24 hours, depending on humidity and thickness of paint.

4 Use craft knife to trim dried paint from around mouth of vase.

"This vase looks like it would be at home in an "upscale" gypsy fortune teller's caravan. The colors and textures are rich and elegant, but the scarf and fringe give the vase a jaunty air.

—Mary Lynn Maloney

5 Fold fabric into a triangle; tie around neck of vase like a scarf, folding under and tucking in all raw fabric edges. When fabric is arranged as you want it, secure it with dabs of glue. Tie each end of hanging fabric in a small knot.

6 Glue 12-inch length of fringe over fabric around the neck of the vase. Cut remaining fringe in half; glue around knotted ends of fabric. ◆

Create It's easy to change the look of this project by simply changing the scarf and beaded trim.

Sunflower Frame

Stuff a portion of the flower centers to create a 3-D look. The painted sunflower is simple to make using a stencil and fabric scraps.

Design by Sharon M. Reinhart

Materials
- Unfinished wooden frame with 4 x 6-inch opening
- ⅛ yard sunflower print fabric
- 1 sheet transparency plastic *or* glass from frame
- Window-cling paints: green, brown, yellow
- Gold liquid leading
- 3⅜ x 5-inch sunflower stencil with 1½-inch-diameter flower center
- Card stock in lattice print or other complementary print or solid
- Satin-finish varnish
- 3-D glue dots
- Medium-weight fusible adhesive
- Fabric glue *or* decoupage medium
- Ballpoint pen
- Stylus
- Tacky craft glue
- Sandpaper
- Sponge paintbrush
- Tack cloth

> *The inspiration for this project began with the colorful sunflower fabric in beautiful shades of yellow, brown and green.*
> —Sharon M. Reinhart

Instructions

1 Remove backing and glass from frame. Lightly sand frame; wipe off dust with tack cloth.

Continued on page 129

Fringy Beaded Choker

Make a fashion statement by adding accent beads
made from colorful fabric strips and decorated
with paint and metallic fibers to a ready-made choker.

Design by Mary Lynn Maloney

Materials

- 18-inch gold wire choker necklace
- 13 gold spacer beads
- ⅛ yard blue-green batik fabric
- 2 plastic drinking straws
- Window-cling paints: blue, green
- Metallic fibers: 48 inches each fine gold cord *and* green braid
- Glue
- Seam sealant
- Skewers *or* knitting needles

Instructions

1 Cut straws into 12 (¾-inch) pieces.

2 Tear fabrics into 1-inch-wide strips; cut stripes into 12 (2-inch) lengths.

3 *Make fabric beads:* Apply light coat of glue around one straw piece; wrap a fabric strip around it, gluing down free end. Repeat to cover all 12 straw pieces with fabric.

4 Thread a few fabric beads onto skewer or knitting needle. Drizzle paints randomly over beads. Suspend skewer with painted beads over edges of box and let beads dry thoroughly.

5 Cut fibers into 4-inch pieces. Holding one green and one gold piece together, wrap them around the center of a bead two or three times and tie in a knot; trim ends to ½ inch. Apply seam sealant to knot; let dry and cut ends. Repeat with all fabric beads.

6 Thread gold and fabric beads alternately onto choker, starting with gold bead. To keep fabric beads from spinning, apply a dot of glue to both ends of gold spacer beads; gently press fabric bead up to spacer beads so knots of fibers face same direction on all fabric beads. Let dry thoroughly. ◆

> I have been collecting batik fabrics lately with no particular project in mind, just because they are so beautiful. I found that they make really nice fabric beads, in a myriad of colors. For this project, I used just the green-blue section of a fabric swatch and learned that the window-cling paint dries to a jewel-like appearance on fabric. The metallic fibers were an appropriate finish for these beads. Wouldn't they be lovely strung on fibers to use in tag art or scrapbooking?
>
> —Mary Lynn Maloney

Create Choose a fabric to match your favorite outfit. It's easy to have a necklace that's perfect for any occasion!

Geometric Key Holder

Mount a painted glass panel on a fabric-wrapped background to create a handy spot for hanging your keys!

Design by Katie Hacker

Materials
- 4 x 12-inch piece craft plywood
- 3½ x 11½-inch piece glass
- Pewter liquid leading
- Window-cling paints: blue, green, yellow
- Denim fabric
- 5 brass cup hooks
- Gem glue
- 2 sawtooth hangers
- Staple gun
- Craft drill with bits
- Craft glue

"Moroccan tiles were the inspiration behind the geometric design used for this piece. Don't worry if your leading lines are not perfect—imperfections add to the folksy quality of the piece."
—**Katie Hacker**

Instructions

1 Using photocopier with enlarging capabilities, enlarge pattern to 133 percent.

2 Lay glass over pattern. Trace over lines with liquid leading, following manufacturer's instructions; let dry.

3 Referring to photo throughout, fill in sections with window colors, adding yellow to corners of panel with circle; blue to outline squares in center panel; and green to outline central motif and fill corners in diamond panel; let dry.

4 Cut 16 x 8-inch piece denim fabric to cover plywood. Wrap fabric around wood; glue long edges to wood on back, then fold ends of fabric to back and secure with staple gun.

5 Attach sawtooth hangers to back of key holder, positioning them ¼ inch from top edge and 8 inches apart.

6 Along bottom edge of board, measure and mark five spots, 2 inches apart. Drill guide holes and screw cup hook into each hole. (Make sure hooks open forward.)

7 Cut pieces of denim to fit behind blue squares and green diamond in design; this will add depth to finished piece. Glue denim in place with gem glue.

8 Apply a thin layer of gem glue on back of colored areas of glass; press glass panel onto center of denim-covered board. ◆

Geometric Key Holder
Enlarge 133%

Sunflower Frame

continued from page 126

2 Apply two or three coats varnish to all surfaces of frame, letting varnish dry between coats.

3 Using cardboard frame insert as a template (or referring to frame opening and adding ¼ inch), trace around insert onto transparency sheet; cut out just inside line. **Optional:** *If you prefer, work on glass insert from frame.*

4 Trace stencil lightly onto transparency plastic. Referring to photo throughout and following manufacturer's instructions, apply liquid leading on top of traced lines of flower and leaves but *not* stem; let dry.

5 Fill petals with yellow paint; add a small amount of brown to inner edges. Trace over stem with green paint; do not fill in center of sunflower or leaves. Let dry.

6 Cut photo to fit in center of flower; tape to back of design.

7 *Fabric leaves:* Apply fusible adhesive to small piece of green fabric (from sunflower fabric). Use stencil to trace two leaves onto bonded side of fabric; cut out. Remove paper backing and adhere leaves to transparency by applying clear-drying fabric glue or decoupage medium to right side of fabric leaf. Adhere leaves to backside of design.

8 Apply fusible adhesive to 4½ x 6½-inch piece of fabric. Fuse fabric to back of a 4½ x 6½-inch piece of lattice-print card stock. Trace template used in step 3 onto plain side of card stock; cut out just inside traced lines. **Note:** *This piece will become the reversible backing sheet for frame. If a thicker backing is needed to hold frame together, fuse fabric to cardboard and then to card stock.*

9 Apply fusible adhesive to a section of fabric from which you will cut the appliqués for frame corners. **Note:** *The fusible adhesive will make it easier to cut the appliqués. Cut six full flower heads from fabric. Remove paper backing.*

10 Apply 3-D glue dot to back of each flower in center. **Note:** *Besides providing adhesive, this helps give the flower dimension.* Apply tacky craft glue to remainder of flower.

11 Referring to photo throughout, position flowers in upper left and lower right corners of frame front, allowing some leaves to extend slightly beyond edges of frame. Using fingernail or stylus tool, burnish around the raised portion of the flower. Smooth out petals so that they adhere to frame. Let dry.

12 Place painted design with photo in frame first, followed by lattice backing sheet. Secure in frame. ◆

Autumn Leaves Frame

Vivid autumn leaves grace the corners of a painted wooden frame.

Design by Sandy L. Rollinger

> *I love autumn, and when I needed to come up with a project using these paints, I just had to create something using colored leaves. I always think of the bright yellow, orange and red leaves gently falling down as spirits of butterflies changing for the last time into their winter attire.*
>
> **—Sandy L. Rollinger**

Materials
- Wooden frame with 5 x 7-inch opening
- ¼ yard muslin
- 2½ x 4¾-inch oak leaf rubber stamp
- Gesso
- Metallic purple acrylic craft paint
- Window-cling paints: amethyst, ruby red, crystal orange, citrine yellow
- Gold liquid leading
- ½-inch or 1-inch flat paintbrush
- Thick white craft glue
- Freezer paper
- Iron
- Hanger *or* frame stand
- Satin-finish clear acrylic spray sealer
- Toothpick

Instructions

1 Iron wrinkles from muslin. Lay muslin on waxed side of freezer paper; iron around edges to hold muslin in place.

Autumn leaves come in many color combinations. Choose the colors that look best with your decor. Try blended, muted colors for a softer look.

Create

2 Using craft brush, apply gesso to leaf stamp. Press stamp gently onto muslin. Repeat to make a total of five leaves, applying gesso each time. Clean stamp thoroughly with water. Let leaves dry for at least 1 hour before proceeding.

3 Trace around leaf shapes and add veins with gold leading; let leaves dry for at least 3 hours, or until completely dry.

4 Working with one leaf at a time, apply window-cling paints to leaves, beginning with yellow on the outer edge, then orange, then red, and finally amethyst, between red and veins.

5 While paints are still wet, use toothpick to pull lighter colors toward darker colors, blending them somewhat. Do not mix too much, or leaf will appear muddy. (You may want to experiment on some practice leaves first.) Pop any bubbles with a toothpick. Let leaves dry overnight.

6 Using small, sharp scissors, carefully cut out each leaf close to gold outline. Touch up any missed areas with paints and let leaves dry completely before continuing.

7 Paint all surfaces of frame with purple paint; let dry, then apply a second coat. Let dry. Spray with acrylic sealer; let dry. Add hanger to back of frame if desired.

8 Referring to photo throughout, glue leaves in upper left and lower right corners of frame. Place glass, photo and backing in frame. ◆

Baby Scrapbook

Toile fabric creates a beautiful memory book for baby. Choose fabric in a muted or pastel color with an appropriate print.

Design by Lorine Mason

Materials
- Spiral-bound scrapbook
- Print fabric: ½ yard *each* of toile *and* a coordinating print
- Polyester fleece batting
- 3¼ x 1¾-inch wooden oval cutout
- Window-cling paints: white *and* color to coordinate with fabric
- Gold liquid leading
- 1 yard coordinating ½-inch grosgrain ribbon
- Poster board
- Hot-glue gun

Instructions

1 Measure height and width of scrapbook's front cover. Using this measurement, cut the following pieces from fabric, batting and/or poster board:

Toile fabric: Add 2 inches to both dimensions and cut two pieces that size for outer covers.

Coordinating print: Add 1 inch to both dimensions and cut two pieces that size for inner covers

Batting: Add 1 inch to both dimensions and cut two pieces that size.

Poster board: Subtract 1 inch from both dimensions and cut two pieces that size; cut two strips 1 inch wide x height of book cover.

2 Lay one piece toile right side down; lay one 1-inch strip poster board on top, ½ inch from right edge. Apply glue to ½ inch of fabric along edge and fold over onto poster board. Repeat with remaining piece of toile and poster-board strip.

3 Glue poster board–reinforced edge of one piece of toile next to the spiral binding on back cover of scrapbook; weight with a heavy object until glue sets. Repeat with remaining piece of toile on front cover.

4 Flip over fabric on back cover, exposing surface of poster board reinforcement strip. Apply glue to top of poster-board strip and lay batting on top of glue. Let dry. Repeat for front cover.

5 Open scrapbook; lay back cover flat, sandwiching batting between toile fabric and book's original cover, smoothing excess batting and fabric over edges to inside of book. Fold corners neatly and glue fabric edges inside book covers.

6 Lay coordinating fabric wrong side up on work surface; lay large poster-board piece in center. Fold excess fabric neatly over edges of poster board and glue in place. Repeat with remaining fabric and poster board.

7 Glue fabric-covered poster board inside scrapbook's back cover, covering edges of toile. Weight with a heavy object until glue is set. Repeat to cover inside front cover.

8 Referring to manufacturer's instructions, outline oval and personalize with gold leading; let dry. Fill design with coordinating paint; let dry. Add dots of white on top of coordinating color; let dry. Glue oval to front of scrapbook as shown.

9 Fold 1 inch of ribbon in half over bottom spiral and glue; weave remaining ribbon in and out of spirals, ending at top of album. Fold ribbon inside album; trim ribbon end at an angle. ◆

> *I love to give gifts I have made especially for the occasion. Choosing the fabric and finding that perfect color and print make the gift a joy to create.*
> —**Lorine Mason**

Create

Personalize this memory book by adding a plaque with the baby's name!

Shabby Chic Pillow

Fray the edges of the floral fabric squares and accent them with painted blossoms to add a cottage feel to your home.

Design by Koren Russell

Materials
- 16-inch square blue pillow
- ¼ yard each of 2 complementary small floral prints, one in blue and one in green
- White liquid leading
- Clear window-cling paint
- Fabric-marking pen
- Fabric glue

Instructions

1 Wash, dry and iron fabric to remove sizing.

2 Cut four 5¼-inch squares from blue print fabric and five from green. Pull threads to fray ¼ inch along each edge of each square.

3 Referring to fabric, pick a flower design and reproduce it on scrap paper to fit in the center of fabric square. **Note:** You can photocopy the fabric and enlarge the image until it is the desired size.

4 Cut out paper pattern; pin to fabric square and trace around it with fabric-marking pen. Referring to photo throughout, go over outline with white liquid leading, dabbing the bottle tip up and down while squeezing to create a textured outline. Repeat on all fabric squares; let dry.

5 Using the tip of the bottle to spread the paint, apply clear paint to flowers inside leading. Let dry.

I love the simple flower and leaf patterns found on many quilting fabrics. I thought it would be fun to use them as an accent and give them some sheen while letting the fabric show through. This project reminds me of something Austin Powers might have in his cottage.
—**Koren Russell**

6 Arrange squares on pillow as shown. Glue in place, applying a dab of fabric glue to back of each fabric square in each corner. Let dry. ◆

Spool Pincushion

A ready-made wooden spool is covered with fabric and embellished with sewing motifs to create a useful accent for the sewing room.

Design by Judi Kauffman

Materials
- 3-inch-wide, ¼-inch-thick wooden heart cutout
- 3 (1 x ¾-inch) wooden spools
- 3 (1-inch) wooden spheres with one flat side
- 1¼-inch wooden thimble
- 3 (1⅝-inch-wide, ⅛-inch-thick) wooden discs
- Ready-made wooden spool pincushion *or* 2 (3¾-inch-diameter, ⅝-inch-thick) wooden discs, 5½-inch wooden dowel and 2 (3½-inch) cardboard circles
- Window-cling paints: black onyx, smoky brown
- Paintbrush
- Vintage fabrics in 4 floral prints
- Assorted embellishments: brass charms, buttons, crocheted flowers, lace motifs, etc.
- Gem glue
- Craft glue
- Fabric glue
- Quilt batting
- Hand-sewing needle *and* thread
- Wood glue (optional)

Instructions

1 Paint heart, spools, thimble, spheres and 1⅝-inch discs with two coats black onyx paint, followed by two coats smoky brown, allowing paint to dry between coats and after final application. **Note:** *Ready-made spool pincushion is already finished. If constructing your own, paint the*

I created this project after I completed my challenge project for this chapter, and I liked the look of fringed fabrics so much that I wanted to continue exploring the possibilities.
—**Judi Kauffman**

3¾-inch disks in the same fashion, after first sanding the edges and wiping off dust.

2 Cut a 6 x 13-inch piece from one fabric. Cut two assorted small squares and rectangles from each of the remaining fabrics; fringe these "patches" by pulling threads from the edges.

3 Cut batting to 5 inches wide; wrap dowel of pincushion (or separate unfinished dowel) with craft batting until bundle measures 3¾ inches in diameter. Tack with glue to hold in place.

4 Cut holes in centers of cardboard circles; slide one onto each end of dowel, making ends for batting roll.

5 Wrap fabric rectangle around batting roll. Using fabric glue, turn under edge at end of fabric and glue to secure; glue this finished fabric edge to roll. Let dry.

6 Using needle and thread, sew running stitch around raw fabric edge at bottom of roll; pull thread ends to gather fabric smoothly over cardboard; knot ends to secure. Repeat

at top of roll. If making your own pincushion, glue ends of dowel in centers of 3¾-inch discs using wood or craft glue.

7 Referring to photo throughout, glue fabric patches and embellishments to fabric surface of pincushion with fabric and gem glues.

8 *Feet:* Glue flat surface of each sphere in center of a 1⅝-inch disc; let dry. Glue discs to bottom of pincushion, spacing them evenly so pincushion rests steadily on ball feet.

9 Arrange heart on its side on top of pincushion; add thimble and stack of spools, leaving room for sliding scissors between heart and spools as shown. When pleased with arrangement, glue heart, thimble and spools in place. ◆

Sunshine & Posies Tissue Box

Wrap a wooden tissue box in bright fabric, then embellish with vellum stickers and shiny glitter.

Design by June Fiechter

Materials
- Wooden tissue box cover
- Bright yellow fabric
- Vellum pastel flower stickers
- Window-cling paints: crystal glitter, orange
- Iridescent ultrafine glitter
- Empty spray bottle
- Fabric glue

Instructions

1 Measure fabric and tissue box in preparation for covering box with fabric.

2 Spread glue over one side of box; press fabric neatly and smoothly into wet glue. Repeat on each side of box, tucking edges under and trimming excess fabric where needed.

3 Glue fabric to top of box, tucking fabric under along straight edges. Insert point of scissors through fabric in center of oval opening; clip to edge of oval. Repeat to clip fabric into 12–15 "petals." Fold fabric over edge of oval opening and securely glue fabric to underside of box cover.

4 Mix orange paint with an equal amount of water in spray bottle. Mist fabric-covered box with mixture; let dry.

5 Press stickers over surface of box, allowing some to extend over edge and around corner. Using crystal glitter paint, outline and embellish stickers, adding random swirls extending from flowers like vines; using tip of crystal glitter paint bottle, add clusters of three dots as shown. Sprinkle with glitter while still wet; let dry. Tap off excess glitter. ◆

> *Isn't yellow a happy color? I chose brightly colored stickers to complement the base color. I plan on using this box in my children's bathroom.*
>
> —June Fiechter

Create

This project can be whimsical, as shown—or make it more elegant simply by changing the background fabric and using sophisticated floral stickers.

Coordinating Papier-Mâché Boxes

Window-cling paint acts as a glaze for the painted floral motifs, adding shine and a bit of dimension to an otherwise flat surface.

Designs by Vicki Schreiner

> *"My inspiration for this project was my love for vintage boxes. Soft Victorian pieces have always caught my eye.*
>
> —Vicki Schreiner

Materials

- 8½-inch *and* 6¾-inch hexagonal papier-mâché boxes with lids
- 2 *or* 3 coordinating cotton fabrics
- 3 yards ½-inch decorative trim
- Tassel
- Laminating liquid
- Fabric adhesive
- Window-cling paints: citrine yellow, crystal pink, emerald green, lilac, peach, smoky brown, white pearl
- Buttercream acrylic craft paint
- Paintbrushes: 1-inch and #4 flats, #4 round, #0 liner
- Graphite transfer paper
- Ballpoint pen
- Stylus
- Toothpick
- Adhesive-backed felt

Covering & Laminating

1 Referring to Fig. 1 throughout, lay lid on wrong side of fabric; trace around it with ballpoint pen. Measure depth of lid side; double that measurement and add ½ inch. Using a ruler, draw a second hexagonal outline that far outside first traced shape. Cut out along second line; trim a notch from each corner (dashed lines).

2 Referring to Fig. 2 throughout, measure one side of box. Add ½ inch to horizontal measurement and 1 inch to vertical measurement; cut three pieces this size from fabric A.

3 Add 1 inch to vertical measurement of box side; cut three pieces this size from fabric B.

4 *Optional:* Cut fabric pieces to cover inside of box.

5 Trace around lid and bottom of box onto wrong side of felt; cut out.

6 Using 1-inch brush, apply fabric to lid with laminating liquid, following manufacturer's instructions. Working on one area at a time, apply liquid to lid surface and back of fabric; press fabric into place, centering it. Press fabric down smoothly, then apply additional laminating liquid until fabric is saturated, brushing out bubbles as you work. Apply laminating liquid to sides of lid and smooth fabric tabs in place; fold edges smoothly over to inside and secure with laminating liquid.

7 In same fashion, apply fabric A pieces to every other side of box, centering them and smoothing excess fabric over edges. Apply fabric B pieces to remaining uncovered sections. Let dry.

8 Apply a second coat of laminating liquid to box and lid; let dry.

Painting

1 Using graphite paper and ballpoint pen or stylus, transfer outer line only of floral motif onto center of box lid.

2 Referring to instructions for base coating throughout ("Painting Techniques," General Instructions, page 174), base-coat entire design with two coats buttercream paint, allowing it to dry between coats. Let dry.

3 Transfer remaining details of pattern onto painted area. ***Note:*** *Do not transfer stippling dots; these are shown for your reference when shading.*

4 Transfer border design around bottom of box; base-coat with two coats buttercream as in step 2.

5 *Base-coat designs:* Using generous amounts of paint and an appropriate-size brush, base-coat each area with two coats of paint as follows, allowing paint to dry between coats.

Leaves: mixture of equal parts emerald green, peach and smoky brown.

Flowers: crystal pink.

Tiny buds: lilac.

Border design: crystal pink.

Let base coating dry thoroughly.

6 Shade leaves by dabbing a generous amount of smoky brown onto areas of leaves indicated by stippling dots, then patting color with brush to soften. In same fashion, shade stippled areas of flowers with lilac. Let dry.

7 Using liner and smoky brown, add vein lines to leaves, vines and tiny buds; using liner and lilac, line each petal. Using stylus dipped in citrine yellow, dot centers of flowers. Using toothpick dipped in white pearl, add a tiny highlight dot to each yellow dot. Let dry.

Create

Peruse painting books to find a floral motif to match your favorite fabrics.

Large Box Border

Finishing

1 Glue trim around lid and bottom of box as shown.

2 Peel backing from felt for lid; press in place inside lid, placing tassel end under felt before pressing it completely into place.

3 Peel backing from remaining felt; press in place on bottom of lid. ◆

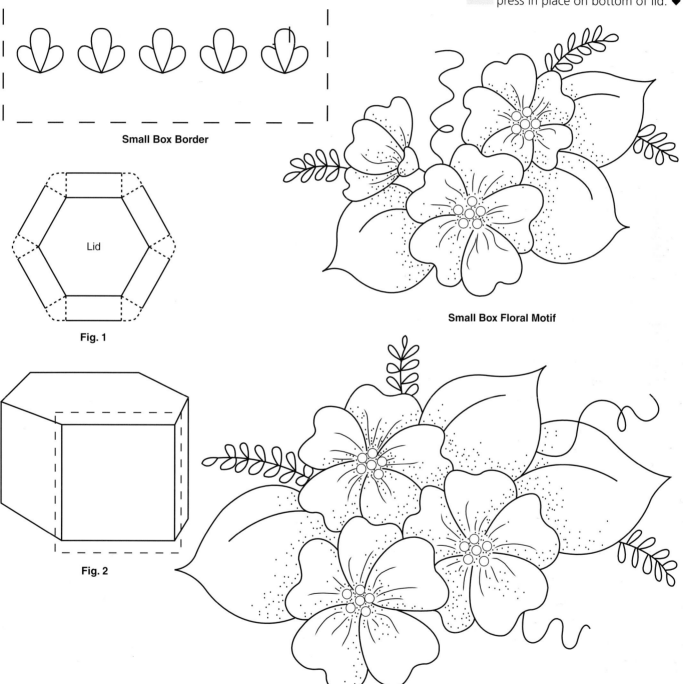

Small Box Border

Lid

Fig. 1

Fig. 2

Small Box Floral Motif

Large Box Floral Motif

PAPER
Markers
Metallic Paint
FELT

We all have felt in our craft closets—from little bits and pieces that we just can't bear to discard to large pieces purchased on sale. Felt combines surprisingly well with materials such as paper and paint, as you'll see from the projects on the following pages!

Trailing Vines Portfolio

The challenge—each designer needs to create a project using the materials we selected (and one or two more items they add).

Design by June Fiechter

"I really enjoyed working with the Fit-it pattern. What a great idea! I've never really imagined decorating a portfolio this way before, but since I've designed this project, I really like the concept. The wool felt is a great contrast in texture to the paper.

—**June Fiechter**

Materials

- Red Castle Fit-It pattern-making software, Vol. 1, for making portfolio/folder (or use template on pages 141 and 142)
- Scrapbook Set papers in pink, lavender *and* purple from Sanook Paper Co.
- Plum die-cut paper circle from Creative Paper Co.
- Natural banyan skeleton leaf from Sanook Paper Co.
- Medium green mulberry paper ribbon from Sanook Paper Co.
- Wheatfields Natural Elements Limited Edition wool felt from National Nonwovens
- LePlume markers from Marvy Uchida: wine, jungle green
- Primary Elements Coloring System #PE-604 (Kit 4) with garnet and ocean wave Polished Pigments, and Simple Solutions #2 for Paper, Plastic and Walls, from Angelwings Enterprises
- Crafter's Pick Memory Mount Glue from API
- Sticky Dots adhesive from Therm-O-Web
- Poster board
- 5 sheets neutral-color card stock (optional)
- Small leaf cluster rubber stamp
- Desired rub-on transfer: picture or words
- ½-inch paintbrush
- Transparent tape
- Transfer paper
- Acrylic sealer/finish

Assemble Portfolio

1 Photocopy template on pages 141 and 142, enlarging as instructed, *or* refer to instructions on pattern-making CD to create pattern for portfolio/folder. **Note:** *Measurements used for flat template are 17.35 inches wide x 22.13 inches high. When folded, this creates a portfolio that measures 9 x 11 inches.* Print out template as directed and piece together along large dashed lines; cut out. **Tip:** *For ease in cutting template, highlight solid cutting lines with a yellow marker before cutting.*

2 Tape pattern onto poster board with transfer paper underneath. Trace all solid and dotted lines. Cut out along solid lines; score on dotted lines. Fold along dotted lines according to software instructions.

3 Glue flaps down inside portfolio. Position one sheet of card stock on portfolio interior over flaps for extra strength, if desired; glue in place. Cut card stock to fit inside side, if needed; do not overlap any dotted lines. Repeat on other inner side.

4 Turn flat portfolio over to outside (front); if desired, glue card stock sheets in center of front and back sections, making sure not to overlap dotted lines. Turn portfolio over.

5 From remaining card stock, cut 1½ x 12-inch strip; glue to inside of spine. Fold in remaining flaps; glue to complete portfolio assembly. Cut 1½ x 5¼-inch piece card stock and

Instructions continued on page 145

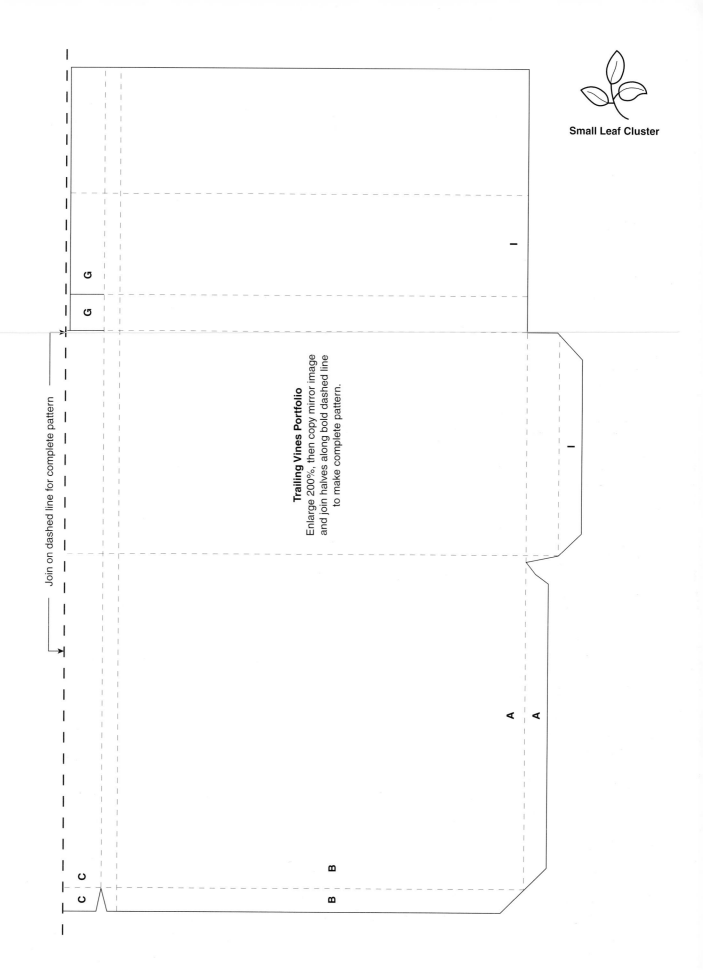

Small Leaf Cluster

Join on dashed line for complete pattern

G
G
G

C
C
C

B
B

A
A

I

I

Trailing Vines Portfolio
Enlarge 200%, then copy mirror image
and join halves along bold dashed line
to make complete pattern.

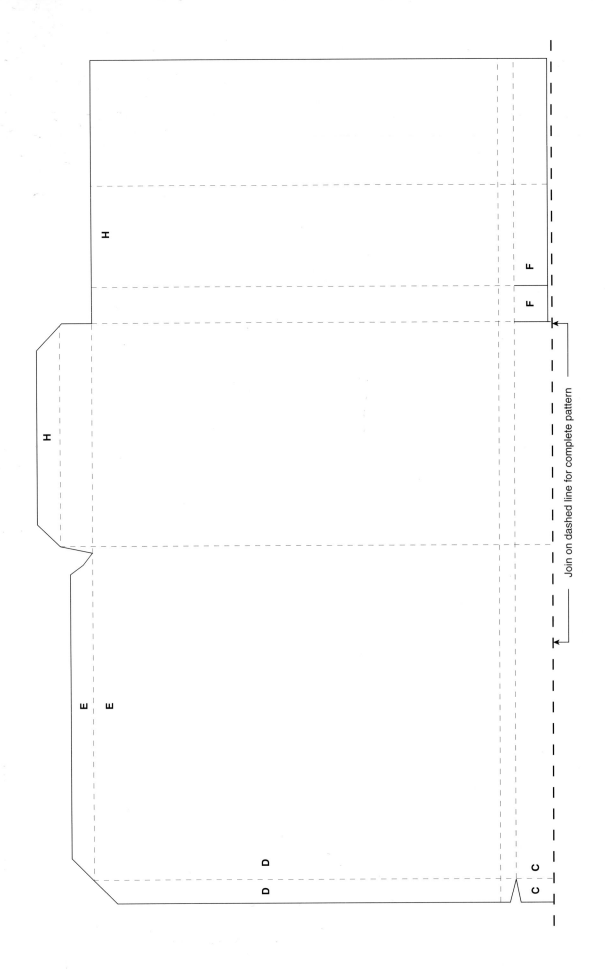

Craft Closet Challenge
Moonscape With Leaves Portfolio

Design by Judi Kauffman

Materials

- Red Castle Fit-It pattern-making software, Vol. 1, for making portfolio/folder (or use template on pages 141 and 142)
- Mulberry paper from Sanook Paper Co.: 4 (12-inch) squares pink with banyan leaves, 4 (12-inch) squares pink textured
- Assorted die-cut paper circles from Sanook Paper Co.
- Olive green mulberry paper ribbon from Sanook Paper Co.
- Natural banyan skeleton leaves from Sanook Paper Co.
- Purple sage Natural Elements Limited Edition wool felt from National Nonwovens
- LePlume markers from Marvy Uchida: wine, burnt umber *and* English red from the Rustic Mountain set
- Primary Elements Polished Pigments powdered pigments from Angelwings Enterprises: gold dust, snapdragon
- Primary Elements Simple Solutions #1 Soft Acrylic Medium from Angelwings Enterprises
- Paintbrush
- Craft knife
- Thick craft glue
- Hot-glue gun
- PPA Matte Acrylic Adhesive Medium from USArtQuest
- Bone folder
- Shell buttons or other dimensional ornaments
- Glue stick

Instructions

1 Photocopy template on pages 141 and 142, enlarging as instructed, *or* refer to instructions on pattern-making CD to create pattern for portfolio/folder. **Note:** *Measurements used for flat template are 17.35 inches wide x 22.13 inches high. When folded, this creates a portfolio that measures 9 x 11 inches.* Print out template as directed and piece together along large dashed lines; cut out.

Tip: For ease in cutting template, highlight solid cutting lines with a yellow marker before cutting.

2 Referring to Fig. 1 and making sure that right sides of paper sheets are facing up, use glue stick to attach four banyan leaf paper sheets to make one large piece of paper, overlapping edges ⅜ inch as shown. Repeat for sheets of pink textured

Continued on page 147

Overlap ⅜"

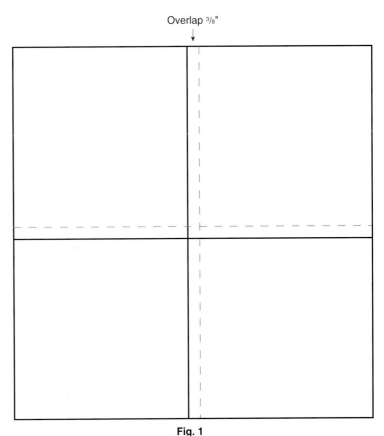

Fig. 1
Overlap 4 pieces of paper by ⅜" as shown
and glue to make a large sheet of paper

Craft Closet Challenge
Family History Portfolio

Design by Mary Lynn Maloney

Materials
- Red Castle Fit-It pattern-making software, Vol. 1, for making portfolio/folder (or use template on pages 141 and 142)
- Dark green heavyweight card stock
- Mulberry paper from Sanook Paper Co.: pinks, purples, creams
- Die-cut mulberry paper circles from Sanook Paper Co.: wine, cream
- Natural banyan skeleton leaves from Sanook Paper Co.
- Mulberry paper ribbon from Sanook Paper Co.: blue, olive green
- Natural Elements Limited Edition wool felt from National Nonwovens: dark green, purple sage
- Primary Elements Polished Pigments powdered pigments from Angelwings Enterprises: sunflower, passion, fern, ocean wave
- Primary Elements Simple Solutions #2 for paper from Angelwings Enterprises
- LePlume markers from Marvy Uchida: teal, wine
- "Looking back" metal eyelet panel
- Eyelet setter with hammer
- Low-tack masking tape
- Double-sided tape
- Craft knife
- Glue stick
- Fabric glue
- Tacky craft glue
- Red Castle bone folder
- Paintbrush

Instructions

1 Photocopy template on pages 141 and 142, enlarging as instructed, *or* refer to instructions on pattern-making CD to create pattern for portfolio/folder. **Note:** *Measurements used for flat template are 17.35 inches wide x 22.13 inches high. When folded, this creates a portfolio that measures 9 x 11 inches.* Print out template as directed and piece together along large dashed lines; cut out. **Tip:** *For ease in cutting template, highlight solid cutting lines with a yellow marker before cutting.*

2 Secure template on heavy green card stock with low-tack tape. Trace with pencil, making sure to indicate scoring lines. Remove template; use ruler and bone folder to score card stock where indicated. Using ruler and craft knife, cut portfolio from card stock but do not fold.

3 Lay portfolio flat to decorate front cover. Referring to photo throughout, use glue stick to adhere 4 x 6-inch pieces of purple, cream and pink mulberry paper in a stair-step formation across the center front of the portfolio.

4 Mix one part sunflower pigment with two parts acrylic solution; use mixture to adhere a skeleton leaf near top right edge of portfolio. Mix fern pigment and solution in same ratio; brush mixture over vein lines of skeleton leaf and onto upper right edge of card-stock cover. While still wet, brush leaf randomly with teal marker, blending teal and green colors together.

5 Tear blue mulberry ribbon to 14-inch length; glue along right side of cover, partially covering painted skeleton leaf. Extend ribbon down

> *As I worked on this piece, I considered what I would keep in the portfolio. I'd recently been looking through my genealogy files and thought they would fit nicely in the pockets of this piece. The beautiful leaves make me think of a family tree and the repetitious circles are a reminder of my connection to the past and the continuity of love and family.*

—**Mary Lynn Maloney**

to what will later become the inside pocket. Glue one wine die-cut circle at top edge of blue ribbon. Mix one part passion pigment with two parts acrylic solution; paint mixture around wine-colored circle.

6 Place one die-cut circle near upper left corner of cover. Mix one part ocean wave pigment with two parts acrylic solution; using circle as a stencil, brush mixture around it. Lift circle, place it in a different position and brush mixture around it again. Repeat one more time. Let dry.

7 Repeat step 6 using mixtures of fern and passion pigments with solution to create a pattern of interlocking rings in upper left portion of cover.

8 Tear a 6-inch piece of olive green mulberry ribbon; glue down at an angle near center top of cover. Tear a triangular piece of pink paper; glue

down over olive green in upper left corner of cover, extending it over left and top edges; brush torn edge with teal marker.

9 Adhere skeleton leaf in upper right quarter of cover, partially covering first leaf and wine circle.

10 Cut purple felt into a curved "slope" to fit across bottom of cover. Using fabric glue, glue bottom edge of felt in place. Tuck three skeleton leaves behind felt and glue leaves in place; brush edges of a wine paper circle with passion mixture from step 7 and tuck edge of circle behind felt. Secure circle and purple felt with fabric glue.

11 Tear olive green ribbon into a shape that will fit within purple felt shape; brush edges with touches of each pigment color, then teal and wine markers.

12 Cut purple paper into desired shape for center motif; cut a piece of green felt in the same shape, but ½ inch smaller all around. Glue felt to paper; glue entire piece in center of cover.

13 Run wine marker around edge of a wine die-cut circle. Glue circle to a piece of pink paper, and tear pink paper into a circle about ¼ inch larger than purple circle; brush torn edges with teal marker. Poke small hole in center of circles and, following manufacturer's instructions, insert "looking back" metal eyelet panel; set with tool and hammer. Glue entire piece in center of green felt.

14 Fold portfolio into final assembled shape, using double-sided tape to adhere flaps where necessary. Store flaps, photos, genealogy information, etc., in portfolio pockets. ◆

Trailing Vines Portfolio
Continued from page 140

glue on end area where portfolio joins together.

6 Using jungle green marker, color outer edges of card stock on front and back covers.

Embellishing & Finishing

1 Mix equal parts garnet and ocean wave paints with #2 solution from coloring system kit; paint outer spine (center) of portfolio. Let dry.

2 Wrap 8½ x 11-inch piece of pink paper over portfolio spine evenly and horizontally; glue in place.

3 Cut lavender sheet into two equal pieces. Using adhesive dots, attach pieces to front and back of portfolio, centered and about 1½ inches from top. **Note:** *Small Leaf Cluster pattern on page 141 can be used instead of*

leaf-design stamp to make the border.

4 Using stamp with leaf design and jungle green marker, add border to lavender sheet.

5 Glue 4 x 6-inch piece purple paper vertically on front of portfolio 2 inches from right edge and top. Cut 3½ x 5½-inch piece felt; glue in center of purple paper.

6 Using pencil, measure and mark a 3 x 3¾-inch rectangle on a 4 x 6-inch piece pink paper; wet pencil lines with a small amount of water and tear. Rub on transfer in center of torn pink rectangle. Attach this piece to center of felt with adhesive dots, curling edges of paper slightly.

7 Wrap paper ribbon around bottom of portfolio. Tie a bow,

pulling right loop free. Cut excess ribbon; secure ribbon to portfolio with glue.

8 Place skeleton leaf on scrap paper; color with wine marker. Position colored leaf on remaining purple paper; trace around it, adding ¼ inch all around. Cut out; glue leaf to purple paper cutout. Let dry.

9 Rub garnet polished pigment over leaf; spray with sealer. Fold leaf in half, right sides facing and open almost all the way. Glue into back of paper ribbon loop.

10 Cut paper circle into fourths; glue one in each corner on front of portfolio. Cut two 1 x 1½-inch pieces of felt; glue to portfolio spine ¼ inch from top and bottom. ◆

Bath Salts in a Bottle

Show off your favorite bath salts in an embellished bottle. Label contents with a pretty handmade tag.

Design by Lisa Galvin

Materials

- Glass bottle with cork stopper
- Epsom salts *or* coarse sea salts
- Soap dye in desired color
- Desired fragrance oil
- Summer sky blue stiffened felt
- Halo blue–gold acrylic paint
- Swirl border rubber stamp
- Disposable plastic fork and bowl
- White card stock
- Cosmetic sponge
- Black brush-style permanent marker
- ³⁄₁₆-inch drive punch and eyelet setter
- White ³⁄₁₆-inch eyelet
- Punchboard
- Mallet
- Scrap paper
- 1½-inch-wide sheer white ribbon
- Decorative fiber thread
- Rocaille beads: clear and light blue seed beads and E-beads
- Beading needle
- Beading thread

Recycled glass food, beverage or apothecary bottles take on relaxing charm when filled with bath salts and adorned with a handmade tag. Fun to make as "girlfriend" or bridal-party gifts, this project is the perfect addition to your next gift basket!

—Lisa Galvin

Instructions

1 Fill bottle with plain epsom salts; empty salts into disposable bowl. Gradually add drops of soap color, mixing with fork until desired color is achieved. Add a few drops of fragrance oil; mix. Pour salts into bottle; insert cork. Discard fork and bowl.

2 Referring to pattern, cut gift tag from card stock; lay tag on scrap paper. Using cosmetic sponge, apply halo blue–gold paint to rubber stamp. Stamp all outer edges of tag. *Note: For best results, dip sponge into paint, then dab off excess before applying color to stamp. For best color, reapply paint before each use.* Let dry.

3 Use brush marker to write name of scent in center of gift tag.

4 Trace around gift tag onto back of felt; cut out ⅛ inch larger all around. Referring to Fig. 1, add

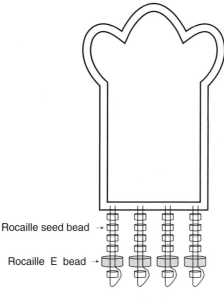

Rocaille seed bead →

Rocaille E bead →

Fig. 1
Attach beaded fringe along edge of felt backing for tag

beaded fringe along bottom edge of felt; whipstitch to secure thread ends.

5 With tag centered on felt, place on punchboard and punch ³⁄₁₆-inch hole at top using drive punch and

mallet. Insert eyelet in hole; set using eyelet setter.

6 Tie ribbon in bow around neck of bottle; trim off excess.

7 Thread assorted decorative threads and fibers through eyelet in gift tag; knot. Slip two thread ends around bow; tie in a knot, hanging tag beneath it. ◆

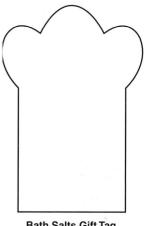

Bath Salts Gift Tag
Cut 1 from card stock

Moonscape With Leaves Portfolio

Continued from page 143

paper, then glue large sheets together wrong sides facing, forming a large, double-sided sheet of paper.

3 Tape template to large double-layer sheet. Cut out on solid lines. Score and fold on dotted lines. Glue flaps with thick craft glue, matching letters when folding for ease of assembly.

4 Cut 3 x 11½-inch strip of felt for spine; set aside.

5 Mix snapdragon powdered pigment with acrylic medium. Using leaf as stencil, paint three felt leaves. Cut out; set aside to dry.

6 Mix gold dust powdered pigment with acrylic medium. Paint four leaves with mixture; move from work surface to another dry area and let dry.

This was one of my favorite challenge projects in the whole book. I love working with paper and have been a fan of felt since childhood, when I used to make dozens of little stuffed animals and ornaments.

—Judi Kauffman

7 Using snapdragon, gold dust or both (separate brushes), lightly brush paint onto die-cut circles (color will remain on top of texture only). Let dry, then color rest of the circles with markers.

8 Using the same paints, lightly brush the portfolio, inside and out. Let dry.

9 Arrange and glue torn paper and die-cut circles on portfolio as shown or as desired. Use acrylic adhesive medium to attach, coat and seal paper pieces. Use thick craft glue to hold felt and skeleton leaves, dabbing tiny dots of glue onto the leaves with your fingertip or a toothpick.

10 Using craft glue, attach felt strip and paper ribbon bow to portfolio spine.

11 Use remaining paper, skeleton leaves and die-cuts to create collage cards to place inside portfolio. Add shell buttons or other dimensional embellishments as desired. ◆

Guest Tote

Fill this decorated canvas bag with mints, scented lotions and tissues to make your overnight guests feel right at home.

Design by Koren Russell

> Hang this purse on the guest room doorknob or place on your guest's pillow. Fill with candies, lotions or goodies to make your guest's stay more comfortable.
> —**Koren Russell**

Materials
- Purse kit
- Metallic bronze fabric paint
- 5 x 9-inch piece moss green felt
- Green felt marker
- Fabric glue
- Paintbrush
- Heavy brown paper bag

Instructions

1 From felt, cut four 1-inch circles; referring to patterns, cut three C's and two V's.

2 Cut 1½ x 2½-inch oval from paper bag; use rest of bag for scrap paper. Write message of your choice on oval.

3 Lay felt pieces right side up on scrap paper. Brush fabric paint onto edges of all pieces; let dry.

4 Referring to photo throughout, glue C's and V's to bottom section of purse; glue bottom circle in place; glue remaining C to flap. Glue only left half of left top circle in place; glue only right half of right top circle in place. Let glue dry.

5 Fill tote (or purse) as desired; slip oval tag under unglued sections of circles. ◆

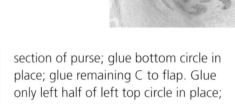

Guest Tote

Apple Canister

Try appliqué on top of felt. It provides a unique padded surface, especially when coated with crackle finish.

Design by June Fiechter

Materials

- Glass canister with wooden lid
- Paper napkin with green apple design
- Metallic craft paints: metallic gold, metallic olive green, metallic bronze
- Brown marker
- Yellow felt
- Decoupage medium
- Crackle medium
- Clear window-cling paint
- Matte acrylic medium
- Stiff paintbrush
- Foam paintbrush
- Pen

" I really like to use crackle finishes in my craft projects. They transform basic into spectacular in a matter of hours. The crackle on this project transforms felt with the rustic look of aged wood or leather. "

—June Fiechter

Instructions

1. Lay canister lid onto felt, top down; trace around it. Cut out felt circle.

2. Using sponge brush, apply decoupage medium to front of wooden lid; press felt circle onto lid.

3. Peel top printed layer from napkin; cut out apple. Coat felt circle with decoupage medium and, referring to photo throughout, press apple into place. Let dry.

4. Paint apple with olive green paint and surrounding felt with gold. Shade around apple with brown marker; feather shading outward with a stiff brush.

5. Apply a coat of decoupage medium over entire front of lid—apple and felt. Let dry.

6. Squeeze a thin layer of clear window-cling paint over entire front surface of lid; let dry.

7. Coat front of lid with a thin coat of crackle medium; let dry.

8. Rub mixture of one part metallic bronze paint and three parts water over crackled surface, immediately wiping off excess. Let dry.

9. Coat lid with matte medium; let dry. ◆

Golden Pears Recipe Box

Metallic paint provides a touch of shimmer and highlight, creating an elegant backdrop for the textured pear motif.

Design by Sharon M. Reinhart

Materials
- 6½ x 4 x 4⅜-inch wooden box with hinged lid
- Acrylic paints: metallic olive, metallic bronze, metallic gold
- Paper-based clay
- ¾ x 1½-inch pear stamp
- White adhesive-backed felt
- Card stock: sage green, ivory
- Double-tipped water-based markers: yellow, dark yellow, sage green, light brown
- Stencil brush
- Small round paintbrush
- Mist spray bottle filled with water
- Tacky craft glue
- Craft knife
- Waxed paper
- Acrylic roller
- Talcum powder
- Sponge
- Tack cloth
- Sandpaper

"The inspiration for the recipe file began with pears and the beautiful transition of colors that they represent."

—**Sharon M. Reinhart**

Use whatever rubber stamp motif fits in with your kitchen decor. How about apples, a rooster, or big, bold sunflowers? Coordinate the background colors with your chosen motif.

Create

Recipe Box

1 Sand box lightly; wipe off dust with tack cloth.

2 Apply one coat metallic olive paint to all surfaces of box, including hardware, using a stencil brush and applying paint in a circular motion. Set box aside to dry.

3 Form three ¾- to 1-inch balls and one 1½-inch ball of paper-based clay; roll out each ball ⅛-inch thick on waxed paper.

4 Lightly dust pear stamp with talcum powder. Press a single pear into each of the smaller pieces of clay; press three pears, overlapping edges, into center of larger piece.

5 Test fit of smaller pieces on front and sides of box and larger piece on lid. "Trim" pieces to fit by pulling

Continued on page 155

X's & O's Frame

Wrap a simple cardboard frame in fancy textured paper. Embellish with rhinestones and felt accents for fun style.

Design by Mary Ayres

Materials
- Square papier-mâché frame
- Purple textured paper
- Lavender solid paper
- Light blue felt
- Clear rhinestones: 7mm, approximately 36 (4.5mm)
- Purple fine-tip permanent marker
- Metallic silver paint
- 1¼-inch (or smaller) square rubber stamp design
- Pinking shears
- White craft glue
- Fabric glue
- Sponge applicator or brush

Instructions

1 Lay frame right side down on wrong side of purple texture paper. Trace around inside and outside edges with pencil. Draw another line 1 inch outside outer line and another line ⅜ inch inside inner line. Cut shape along inner- and outermost lines. Clip paper diagonally at corners from edge to frame outlines.

2 Dilute craft glue with a little water. Brush mixture onto frame front and adhere to wrong side of paper, making sure frame is inside drawn frame shape. Brush glue onto wrong side of extended edges of paper and fold over to back of frame, one at a time, folding outer corners neatly.

3 Dab silver paint onto stamp with sponge or brush applicator; stamp image onto lavender paper. Let dry.

4 Using purple marker, outline shapes of stamped image with tiny purple dots; let dry.

5 Referring to photo throughout, cut square shape from stamped paper, cutting close to edges of stamped design. Glue to light blue felt. Using pinking shears, cut out felt square close to edge of paper square. Glue felt-and-paper square to frame at center bottom.

6 Using pinking shears, cut ¼-inch-wide strips from felt; cut strips in random lengths. Glue around inner and outer edges of frame ¼ inch from edge, leaving about ¼ inch between strips and in corners.

7 Glue large rhinestone in center of stamped design; glue small rhinestones in outer and inner corners of frame, in corners of paper square and in spaces between felt strips. ◆

Create

Vary the background paper to fit the photo. Experiment with different decorative-edge scissors to create a unique trim. Glue on metallic studs instead of rhinestones.

In trying to decide what I would create for this project, I checked out scrapbooking papers in my local art store and found this unique crinkled-look paper that I thought would make a great background for a frame. Because the paper was so busy, I chose simple elements for the remainder of the design.

—**Mary Ayres**

Buttons & Blocks Greeting Set

Paper and felt combine in a unique way to create a very special greeting card with a matching tag.

Designs by Katie Hacker

Materials
- 4¼ x 7-inch blank white greeting card
- 2⅛ x 4¼-inch white card stock hangtag
- Purple felt
- Assorted magenta patterned papers (samples used four patterns)
- Magenta metallic acrylic paint
- Small paintbrush
- 4 (¾-inch) purple buttons
- Purple calligraphy marker
- 7 inches sheer pink *or* orchid ⅝-inch ribbon

Card

1 Cut three 2-inch squares from felt. Paint edges of each square with magenta paint; let dry.

2 Paint areas of three buttons for highlights; let dry.

3 From one patterned paper, cut a 2⅝ x 7½-inch rectangle; from another, cut a ⅝ x 1¾-inch rectangle; from another, cut a 1½-inch square, and from another, two ⅝-inch squares.

4 Referring to photo throughout, glue large paper rectangle across center of card. Glue felt squares, evenly spaced, across center of paper rectangle. Glue small paper rectangle vertically on left side of left felt square; glue larger paper square in center of center felt square; glue smaller paper squares in opposite corners of right felt square. Weight card with a heavy book until glue is dry.

5 Glue buttons to felt squares as shown; let dry.

6 Write "thinking of you" or desired sentiment on card with calligraphy marker.

Gift Tag

1 Cut 2-inch square from felt. Paint edges with magenta paint; let dry.

2 Paint a portion of one button to highlight it; let dry.

3 From one patterned paper, cut a 1¹⁵⁄₁₆ x 2¹¹⁄₁₆-inch rectangle; from another, cut a 1⅛-inch square.

4 Referring to photo throughout, glue paper rectangle in center of tag. Glue felt square in center of paper rectangle. Glue paper square on the diagonal in center of felt square. Weight tag with a heavy book until glue is dry.

5 Glue button in center of paper square; let dry.

6 Write "for you" or desired sentiment on bottom of tag with calligraphy marker.

7 Loop sheer ribbon through hole in tag and tie in a bow or simple overhand knot; trim ends as desired. ◆

Choose colors and felts to coordinate with seasons or special occasions. Try pastels for baby showers, bright primary colors for birthdays and shades of orange for autumn.

An unexpected card at an unexpected time is a sweet way to say hello to a friend. I like to make cards for special occasions, so I try to create designs that can be changed just a little to suit a variety of occurrences. Add bows to the squares on this "thinking of you" card and you have instant birthday packages for a birthday card. Use pastel colors and you have baby blocks for a baby shower card.

—Katie Hacker

Mod Circles Greeting Card & Envelope

Layer brightly colored circles of paper and felt to create a funky, modern look. Add a vellum envelope so that the card is visible.

Design by Mary Lynn Maloney

Materials
- 8⅝ x 7½-inch piece white matte card stock
- Metallic markers: purple, orange
- Fine-point metallic gel pens: pink, blue
- 4 x 5-inch pieces handmade multicolor papers: yellow/pink, yellow/green
- 4 x 5-inch pieces felt: hot pink, bright green, bright yellow
- Pearlescent fabric paints: magenta, turquoise
- 12-inch square yellow vellum
- Circle template
- Paintbrush
- White craft glue

Instructions

1 Score and fold card stock in half to make 3¾ x 8⅝-inch card.

2 Referring to photo throughout, use purple marker and ruler to draw stripe down opening edge of card. Let dry, then add pink, blue and orange stripes with marker and gel pens.

3 Using template, cut circles from handmade papers: 2-inch and 1-inch from yellow/pink; 2¼-inch and 1⅜-inch from yellow/green paper. Set aside.

4 Using template, cut circles from felt: 2-inch, 1½-inch and 1-inch from bright green; 1½-inch, 1-inch and ⅝-inch from bright yellow; 2⅛-inch, 2-inch and 1¾-inch from hot pink.

5 Paint small circle of magenta fabric paint off-center in each of two largest yellow felt circles and smallest circle of bright green felt. Paint small circle of turquoise fabric paint off-center on 1¾-inch circle of hot pink felt. Let dry.

6 Using craft glue, glue hot pink felt circle with blue dot on larger yellow/green paper circle; glue larger bright yellow felt circle with magenta dot on larger circle of yellow/pink paper; glue smaller yellow/green paper circle onto 2⅛-inch hot pink felt circle; glue smaller yellow/pink paper circle to largest bright green felt circle.

7 Glue paper/felt circles and 1-inch yellow and green felt circles to front of card as shown.

8 Lay closed card on vellum sheet; fold vellum so that it wraps around card like envelope. Cut edge for envelope flap in a freeform curve.

9 Close ends of envelope by gluing remaining green felt circle over one end and magenta felt circle over the other end; glue remaining ⅝-inch yellow felt circle to green felt circle on front of envelope. ◆

I love the clean, bright colors and simple shapes used in the clothing, accessories and interior designs of the 1960s. This card and envelope are a nod to mod!
—**Mary Lynn Maloney**

Metallic Elegance Note Cards

Combine several types of materials to create unique collages. Choose bright copper for a masculine look or soft gold for something more feminine.

Designs by Chris Malone

Materials

Each Card
- 5 x 7-inch ivory note card
- Black felt
- Gold leafing pen
- Paintbrush
- Craft glue
- Embroidery needle
- Deckle-edge scissors

Gold Card
- 2½ x 4-inch torn rectangle of ivory handmade paper with gold fibers
- 3½ x 5½-inch piece metallic gold perforated paper for cross-stitch

- Emerald green pearl acrylic paint
- 6mm gold rose bead
- 4 (⁷⁄₁₆-inch) gold leaf beads
- Metallic gold embroidery floss

Copper Card
- 4 x 8½-inch piece copper-colored paper
- 2 x 6½-inch piece ivory paper net
- Copper metallic acrylic paint
- 11 or 12 copper and brass-plated E-beads
- Metallic copper embroidery floss

Collage is a fun process of combining and layering materials, and a palette of paper, felt and paint seemed a perfect recipe for this technique. Lumiere is a beautiful metallic acrylic paint, so I selected metallic papers, pen, beads and floss to enhance the effect. A handmade note card is a special treat for the recipient and a wonderful item to have on hand.

—**Chris Malone**

Gold Card

1 Dab green paint onto 1½-inch square of black felt; let dry.

2 Soften edges of felt by holding edge in two spots and pulling until edge is distorted; continue around square.

3 Press gold leafing pen onto felt; dab randomly; let dry.

4 Trim edges of gold perforated paper with deckle-edge scissors, working scissors back and forth to produce an uneven line.

5 Thread embroidery needle with 3 strands separated from a length of gold floss. Referring to photo throughout, stem-stitch a slightly curved line ¾ inch long and ending in center of felt square. Sew rose bead at end of stem line in center of felt square; sew leaf beads radiating out from rose bead.

6 Layer gold perforated paper, ivory paper and felt on front of card as shown; glue in place.

Copper Card

1 Complete steps 1–4 as for gold card, substituting a 2-inch felt square for the 1½-inch, copper paper for the gold perforated paper, and copper paint for the green.

2 Thread embroidery needle with 6 strands separated from a length of copper floss. Referring to photo throughout, sew E-beads to painted area of felt in a scattered pattern, attaching them individually or in pairs, and letting floss show as much as possible. Knot floss on back of felt and bring needle through to front. Trim floss, leaving 2-inch tail hanging from bead cluster.

3 Layer copper paper, ivory paper net and felt on front of card as shown; glue in place. ◆

Create

Look for unusual material when creating collage art. Pieces of metallic screen, loosely woven fabrics, beads and handmade papers all make an impact when combined.

Golden Pears Recipe Box

Continued from page 150

small pieces of clay from edges with fingers; cracks and uneven texture are desirable. Use craft knife or pin to cut shallow V shapes along edges to create additional "cracks" and "tears" in clay; lay pieces flat and set aside to air-dry.

6 *Paint stamped clay medallions:* Using a circular motion and stencil brush, apply gold paint to entire clay pieces; follow with bronze on a small portion of pear and olive on top portion of pear, on leaves and stem, using small paintbrush to apply color to leaves and stem. Randomly apply a light coat of olive to the entire piece; if olive seems too dark, lighten by applying more gold. Finish all edges of clay pieces with bronze paint.

7 Glue pieces to box, gluing one with three pears to top of lid and remaining pieces to front and sides of box. Glue one piece in place at a time, and top with a protective sheet and then a weight to help secure.

8 Cut four 1¼-inch circles from felt. Sponge each with olive paint; let dry.

9 Remove backing from felt circles. Apply one in each corner on bottom of recipe box.

Recipe Cards

1 For each recipe card, cut ivory card stock to measure 3¼ x 5⅞ inches; for each divider, cut sage card stock to measure 3⅜ x 5⅞ inches.

2 Apply colors from markers to pear rubber stamp, applying lightest color first and working your way to darkest. Lightly mist stamp with water, then press onto left side of recipe card. Clean stamp on a wet cloth and repeat application of color with markers between stampings. ***Note:*** *You can achieve different effects depending on how much water is misted; you can also alter the effects by moving the stamp around after misting them, allowing the colors to run.* ◆

Polka-Dot Candle Lamps

White paper dots add fun and whimsy to daisy-bordered lamp shades.

Design by Samantha McNesby

Materials
- 2 battery-operated brass candle lamps with white plastic "candles"
- Acrylic craft paints: medium pink, medium blue
- White *or* ivory pearlescent paint
- Felt: 9 x 12-inch sheet white; scraps of light pink, light blue
- 1 sheet white card stock
- 2 (4½-inch) paper *or* fabric mini shades for candle lamps
- Foam brush
- Crumpled plastic wrap *or* plastic bag
- Thick white craft glue *or* hot-glue gun
- Standard round hole punch
- Markers: pink, blue

Pink Lamp Shade

1 Paint one lamp shade with two coats pink paint, allowing paint to dry between coats.

2 Blend a mixture of equal parts pink and pearlescent paint. Load foam brush with mixture. With crumpled plastic at hand, paint one section of plastic candle at a time, then blot with plastic, allowing some of the base color to show through. Let dry.

3 Using foam brush, apply a coat of blended pearl-pink mixture to lamp shade; let dry.

4 Referring to patterns, trace 13 daisies onto white felt and 13 daisy centers onto pink felt; cut out. Glue centers onto daisies; glue daisies around bottom edge of lamp shade.

5 Punch about 50 holes from card stock; glue paper dots to lamp shade, spacing them evenly and using more or fewer dots as needed. Using pink marker, add a dot in center of each card-stock dot.

6 Place shade on lamp.

Blue Lamp Shade
Substitute blue paint, felt and marker for pink. ◆

Enlarge the daisies and the dots to cover larger lamp shades. Try creating these in shades of yellow and orange for sunny cheer.

Create

Daisy Center

Daisy

The big challenge here was using both paper and felt. Most projects call for one or the other, but not both! I decided I wanted a whimsical polka-dot and flowers look, and using a hole punch reduced my cutting time dramatically! I used Radiant Pearls as a shimmering finish for the shades and as a glimmering paint extender for the candles to give the project a soft pearlescent glow.
—Samantha McNesby

Embossed Roses Hanger Set

When you give a wearable as a gift, include a covered hanger to match. Cleaning instructions are on the attached tag.

Design by Lorine Mason

Materials
- 2 heavy-duty brass-plated hangers
- Felt embossed with rose pattern: ¼ yard each beige *and* burgundy
- Metallic acrylic paints: green, copper
- ¼-inch copper-wired ribbon
- Card stock
- Green felt-tip marker
- Scallop-edge scissors
- Paintbrush
- Pins
- Fabric glue
- ⅛-inch round hole punch
- Sewing machine
- Matching sewing thread

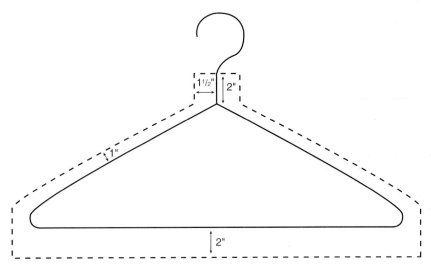

Fig. 1

Beige Hanger Cover

1 *Make pattern:* Referring to Fig. 1, lay hanger on a sheet of newspaper. Place a mark at center point of hook. Measure and trace a line 1½ inches outside center point on each side and 2 inches up from center marking. Continue to trace a line 1 inch from sides and 2 inches from bottom of hanger. Cut out pattern.

2 Using pattern, cut two pieces beige felt and two pieces burgundy for each hanger cover.

3 Lay beige pieces together right sides facing; sandwich between

Continued on page 159

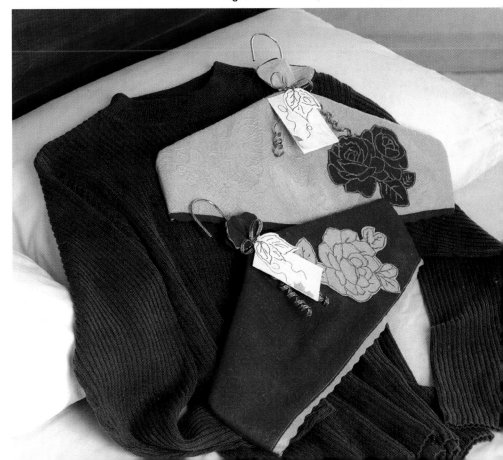

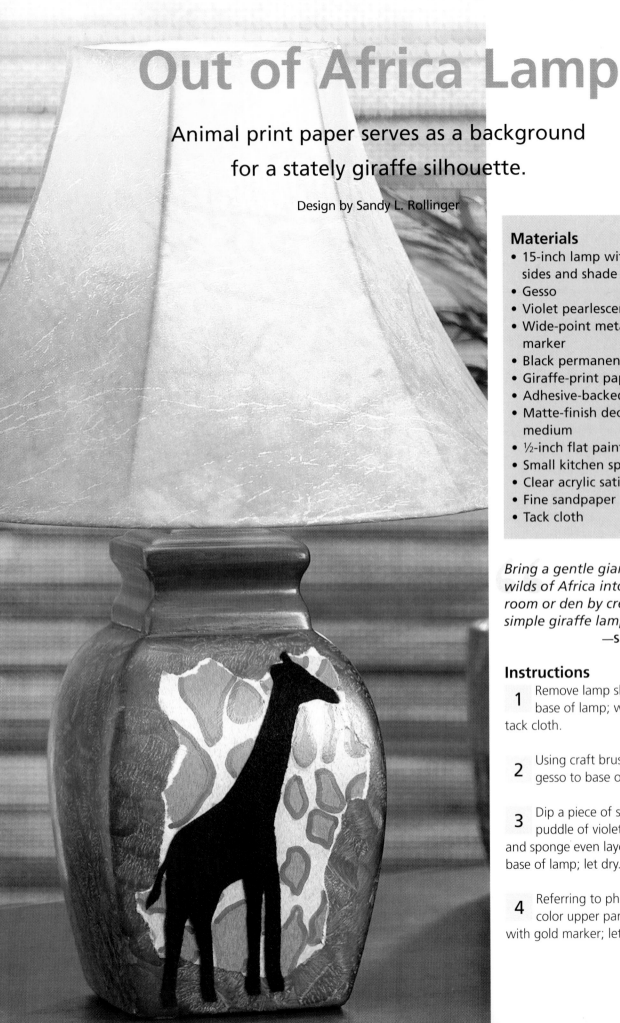

Out of Africa Lamp

Animal print paper serves as a background
for a stately giraffe silhouette.

Design by Sandy L. Rollinger

Materials

- 15-inch lamp with fairly flat sides and shade
- Gesso
- Violet pearlescent paint
- Wide-point metallic gold marker
- Black permanent marking pen
- Giraffe-print paper
- Adhesive-backed black felt
- Matte-finish decoupage medium
- ½-inch flat paintbrush
- Small kitchen sponge
- Clear acrylic satin-finish spray
- Fine sandpaper
- Tack cloth

Bring a gentle giant from the wilds of Africa into your living room or den by creating this simple giraffe lamp.

—Sandy L. Rollinger

Instructions

1 Remove lamp shade. Gently sand base of lamp; wipe off dust with tack cloth.

2 Using craft brush, apply a coat of gesso to base of lamp; let dry.

3 Dip a piece of sponge into a puddle of violet pearlescent paint and sponge even layer of paint onto base of lamp; let dry.

4 Referring to photo throughout, color upper part (neck) of lamp with gold marker; let dry.

5. Spray lamp base with clear satin-finish spray; let dry.

6. Trace giraffe onto wrong side of adhesive-backed felt; cut out.

7. Tear a piece of giraffe-print paper a bit smaller than one side of lamp base. Tear out bits of paper around edges for an uneven effect. Outline giraffe spots with gold marker; let dry.

8. Apply decoupage medium to back of paper; position on one side of lamp base. Apply a thin coat of medium over front of paper, smoothing wrinkles. Let dry.

9. Peel backing from felt giraffe; press onto giraffe paper on lamp base as shown.

10. Replace lamp shade and bulb. ◆

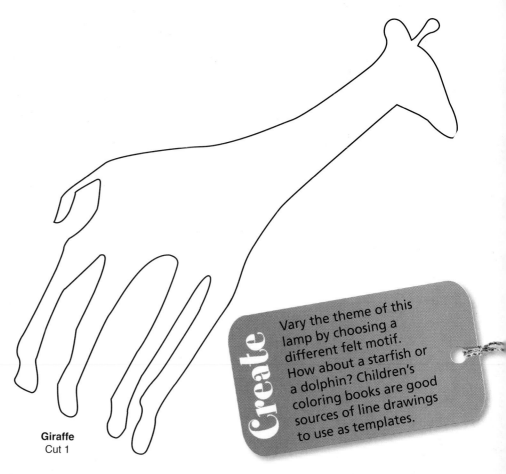

Giraffe
Cut 1

Create — Vary the theme of this lamp by choosing a different felt motif. How about a starfish or a dolphin? Children's coloring books are good sources of line drawings to use as templates.

Embossed Roses Hanger Set
Continued from page 157

wrong sides of burgundy pieces. Leaving 1-inch section open at center top and using matching thread and ½-inch seam allowance, machine-stitch seam along sides of hanger cover. Trim seam allowance to ¼ inch. Turn right side out and press, taking care not to press out the embossed pattern.

4. Pin beige felt to adjacent burgundy felt along bottom of hanger cover, leaving bottom open. Machine-stitch burgundy felt to beige felt ½ inch up from bottom edge and continue stitching around hanger cover, leaving bottom open.

5. Trim beige felt close to stitching. Trim burgundy felt with scallop-edge scissors for decorative finish; trim top edge of hanger cover, rounding corners if desired.

Special gifts are for special people. Your gift will be remembered each time that favorite outfit is removed from a beautiful hanger.
—Lorine Mason

6. From remaining felt remnants, cut a burgundy cluster of embossed flowers. Glue to front of beige hanger cover as shown.

7. Highlight embossed floral design with paints, using copper on flower and green on leaves; add a second coat as needed. Let dry.

8. Slip hanger inside cover. Tie ribbon in bow around neck of hanger.

9. *Tag:* Cut 2 x 6-inch piece card stock; fold in half. Using markers, write purchase and cleaning information inside tag. Cut out simple leaf shapes; punch hole in top of tag and leaves. Thread ribbon though holes; tie tag and leaves around hanger. Curl ribbon ends.

Burgundy Hanger Cover
Substitute beige for burgundy felt and vice versa. ◆

LEATHER & SUEDE
Acrylic Paint
Rub-On Transfers
FLORALS

Create one-of-a-kind projects with an unexpected combination of craft materials. Add your personal touch by substituting materials you already have on hand!

Seashore Bookend

The challenge—each designer needs to create a project using the materials we selected (and one or two more items they add).

Design by June Fiechter

Books are some of the most interesting decorating accessories. Even if you don't read them, books give any house a homey, lived-in look. This bookend is a simple accent to help display your books. Leather is fun to design with and gives this bookend a warm feel. I have always been impressed with the "laced-up" concept, so I opted to incorporate it here with the leather lace. Close your eyes and hold this bookend up to your ear (OK, use some imagination now). Can you hear the ocean?

—June Fiechter

Materials

Each Bookend

- Wooden bookend #24283 from Walnut Hollow
- White acrylic paint
- Large suede trim pieces from The Leather Factory: beige, medium brown
- 1 yard tan leather suede lacing from The Leather Factory
- Tulip Premium seashore-theme rub-on transfers #MPD98 and #MPD105 from Duncan Crafts
- Sprigs of assorted small dried florals and greenery
- Craft drill with bits
- ½-inch sponge paintbrush
- Fabric adhesive
- Medium-grit sandpaper
- Tack cloth

Instructions

1 Paint bookend white; let dry. Sand lightly with the grain to expose wood in some areas; wipe off dust with tack cloth.

2 Referring to photo throughout, measure and *lightly* mark a vertical line on each side of the upright ½ inch from edge. Beginning ½ inch from top, drill a hole every ½ inch along this line. Sand as needed.

3 Lay a corner of beige leather sheet into corner of bookend, matching straight edges; trace along curve on back of leather. Cut out; check fit on bookend. Cut a matching piece for the other side.

4 Referring to manufacturer's instructions, transfer words from rub-on transfer sheet—"Near the sea we forget to count the days"—onto leather for front of bookend about 1⅜ inches from bottom edge and ⅞ inch from inner edge. Glue leather pieces to front and back of bookend.

5 Cut leather lacing in half. Tie a knot about ½ inch from one end of one piece. Beginning at bottom, thread lace through holes and over edge of bookend, leaving knot visible at bottom of bookend. Glue lace in top hole; when glue is dry and leather lacing is secure, trim off excess flush with surface of bookend that will face books. Repeat on other side of bookend.

6 Set bookend on medium brown suede; trace around bottom.

Cut out leather and glue to bottom of bookend.

7 Arrange and glue greenery and dried floral sprigs in corner of bookend.

8 Cut images of two identical scallop shells from transfer sheet; peel backing from both pieces. Place shells together, wrong sides facing, and rub gently on fronts to join shell transfers.

9 Remove the stiffer plastic burnishing sheet from both shells. Work carefully as shells are very fragile at this point. Place one piece of the plastic on a towel and give it a slight bowl shape by burnishing it in the center only with transfer stick. Apply glue to the outer (convex) surface and carefully attach the shell transfer, giving it the appearance of a real, dimensional scallop shell. Let dry.

10 Cement shell in among greenery as shown. ◆

Seaside Stories Bookend

Design by Judi Kauffman

"For me, this challenge project was built around the seashell transfers and the notion that I could make something that looks like it came straight from the beach to the bookshelf. I even added texture medium to the sand-colored paint so it would feel gritty to the touch.
—**Judi Kauffman**

Materials
Each Bookend
- Wooden bookend #24283 from Walnut Hollow
- Texture medium
- Acrylic craft paints: light tan, bright violet, purple, fawn
- Sponge brush
- Hot pink leather lacing from The Leather Factory
- Medium brown suede from The Leather Factory
- Tulip Premium seashore-theme rub-on transfers #MPD98 and #MPD105 from Duncan Crafts
- Assorted small seashells
- Faux sea grass
- Natural raffia
- Craft glue
- Adhesive-backed cork or felt protective patches

Instructions

1 Paint bookend with fawn paint; let dry. Add second coat if needed for complete, even coverage.

2 Mix texture medium with light tan paint. Using sponge brush, dab it onto all surfaces of bookend except bottom. While paint is still wet, randomly sponge bright violet and purple paints over tan surfaces. Add additional light tan if needed. Let dry.

3 Sponge bright violet and purple paints onto suede, working for the same mottled look as the bookend; let dry.

4 Following manufacturer's instructions, rub two large shell transfers onto painted surface of suede. Cut out transfer images leaving a curved border of suede around some of the edges.

5 From remaining painted suede, cut about 15 narrow, curved strands for grass (2–6 inches long); cut also seven pieces from leather lacing, each about 2 inches long, with ends tapered to a point.

6 Referring to photo throughout, arrange and glue suede pieces with shell transfers to flat surface of bookend. Add layers of painted suede grass and pieces cut from pink lacing. Glue faux sea grass and raffia in front. Arrange and glue real shells in front of grass on base of bookend, adding more sea grass between and around shells as desired.

7 Place cork or felt patches on bottom of bookend.

Note: *If you wish, write the date when and location where you collected the real shells on the back or bottom of your bookends.* ◆

Craft Closet Challenge
Suede Waves Bookend

Design by Mary Lynn Maloney

"This simple bookend would be a nice, useful gift for anyone who appreciates the soothing sights and sounds of the seashore. It's also an unexpected place to display a few seashells."

—Mary Lynn Maloney

Materials

Each Bookend

- Wooden bookend #24283 from Walnut Hollow
- Metallic turquoise pearlescent acrylic paint
- 9 x 12-inch pieces suede from The Leather Factory: beige, medium brown
- 2 yards *each* beige *and* turquoise lacing from The Leather Factory
- Tulip Premium seashore-theme rub-on transfers #MPD98 and #MPD105 from Duncan Crafts
- Sponge brush
- Dried Spanish moss
- 4 small seashells
- Leather cement
- Tacky craft glue

Instructions

1 Referring to photo throughout, paint bookend with turquoise paint; let dry.

2 Using the curve of the bookend as a guide, cut a large piece of medium brown suede to cover part of the curved face of the bookend; glue down with leather cement. Cut a randomly curved, wavy-edge piece from beige; glue it in place, overlapping brown piece. Continue adding suede pieces, alternating colors and varying shapes, until face of bookend is covered. Repeat on other side of bookend.

3 Choose a mixture of large and small rub-on transfers; referring to manufacturer's instructions, transfer three or four motifs to suede near inner corner. Gently press with finger to insure that images are firmly in place. Repeat on other side of bookend.

4 Cut 12 inches turquoise lacing; using leather cement, glue around bottom edge of curved face of bookend, trimming off excess. Cut a 6-inch piece of turquoise lacing; cement in a wavy line over beige suede; trim excess, and repeat on other side of bookend.

5 Cut 20 inches beige lacing; using leather cement, glue in a wavy line around bottom of bookend; trim excess.

6 Gather a small bundle of Spanish moss. Glue to bookend vertically, up corner between the curved face and vertical upright, partially overlapping transfers. Use tacky glue to glue a few small shells in front of Spanish moss and seashell transfers. Repeat on other side of bookend. ◆

By the Sea Wastepaper Basket

Rub-on transfers resemble ceramic tiles in this easy-to-create project. Add a touch of the beach to your home in no time at all.

Design by Lisa Galvin

> " *I love finding bare or solid painted surfaces in the clearance aisles at discount stores! Like a canvas screaming for embellishment, this project is a perfect example of taking something very ordinary, a painted (or unfinished) wooden wastebasket, and transforming it into a beautiful home decor piece—a perfect addition to your guest bath or sunroom!* "
>
> —Lisa Galvin

Materials
- Small wooden wastebasket
- Cream-color satin-finish paint (optional)
- Antique gold metallic acrylic paint
- Matte-finish acrylic sealer
- Paintbrushes: ⅜-inch flat, #1 fine tip, bristle brush
- 2 (5-inch) squares tan deerskin *or* faux suede
- Rotary cutter with 45mm wave blade
- Self-healing mat
- Straightedge
- 2 lighthouse rub-on transfers with seagulls
- Matte-finish decoupage medium
- 7 x 12-inch piece medium-weight watercolor paper *or* poster board
- 3–4 stems dried flowers with greenery
- Dried reindeer moss
- Seashells
- Assorted clear glass pebbles
- Clear-drying craft glue

Instructions

1 If wastebasket is unfinished, paint with cream paint; let dry.

2 Using flat paintbrush, paint top flat edge of waste basket with two or three coats of antique gold paint; let dry. Brush all newly painted surfaces with sealer; let dry completely.

3 Referring to photo throughout and following manufacturer's instructions, transfer lighthouse images onto watercolor paper, leaving a paper border around images. Brushing in different directions for best results, use bristle brush to apply decoupage medium over transfers and plain paper around edges; let dry completely.

4 Cut out transfers; adhere one to center of each leather piece; let dry.

5 Working with one piece of leather at a time, place a piece on cutting mat. Using straightedge and rotary cutter fitted with wave blade, trim leather, leaving a ½-inch border around transfers. Glue leather to wastebasket as shown; let dry.

6 Apply assorted coordinating transfers to other areas of wastebasket as shown or as desired. Using fine-tip paintbrush, paint additional small seagulls in background at top, if desired.

7 Glue moss, shells, greenery, pebbles and other embellishments at base of wastebasket as shown. ◆

Cheery Cherry Wall Plaque

Leather lacing adds an eye-catching accent to the edges of this frame. Choose a color to highlight one of the colors in the rub-on transfer.

Design by Sharon M. Reinhart

"The inspiration for the cherry plaque began with the actual rub-on design. The paint colors chosen were taken from the design itself.
—**Sharon M. Reinhart**

Materials
- 5 x 7-inch wooden plaque
- Acrylic paints: tan, green
- Cherries rub-on transfer
- 45 inches natural-color leather lacing
- ¾-inch white silk flower with three green silk leaves
- Tacky craft glue
- 3-D foam tape
- Two flat-back thumbtacks
- Spray acrylic sealer
- Foam paintbrush
- Craft stick
- Sandpaper
- Tack cloth
- Painters tape

Instructions

1 Sand plaque lightly; wipe off dust with tack cloth.

Try substituting rope for leather lacing and use nautical rub-ons for a seaside accent. Glue on a small seashell or starfish for added dimension.

Create

2 Apply two coats tan paint to entire plaque, letting paint dry between coats; apply one coat to heads of thumbtacks.

3 Paint beveled edge of plaque green, masking off other areas as needed. **Note:** *If you choose a different shape of plaque or a different rub-on, let them determine the placement of your accent color. Let dry.*

4 Cut design from transfer sheet; remove backing sheet. Center design on plaque and, referring to manufacturer's instructions throughout, burnish entire design with craft stick until it is completely transferred. Carefully lift off top sheet.

5 Add smaller components from rub-on design in corners for accents or as desired.

6 Determine length of lacing needed to go around edges of plaque. Applying tacky glue to one side of lacing and working with a small portion at a time, adhere lacing around edge, beginning and ending at center bottom and using a craft knife to cut ends neatly and butt them together.

7 Spray front of plaque with sealer; let dry.

8 *Attach silk blossom and leaves over transferred leaves:* To give leaves dimension, apply a little piece of 3-D foam tape behind each silk leaf and glue only to the center of the leaf cluster. Glue blossom in center of leaves.

9 Fold 12-inch piece of leather lacing in half; tie knot 1 inch from fold. Using tacks, attach ends to back of plaque ½ inch from top edge and 1 inch apart. Trim off excess lacing. ◆

Floral Garden Book Cover

Decorating a ready-made leather book cover is as easy as rubbing on a pretty floral transfer.

Design by Sherian Frey

Materials
- 5 x 8-inch leather book cover
- Pansies rub-on transfers
- Gold acrylic craft paint
- Clear acrylic finish for leather
- 12–18 inches ⅜-inch green satin ribbon
- Silk pansy with leaf
- Paintbrush
- Tacky craft glue

Instructions

1 Open book cover and lay flat, outer surface facing you. Referring to photo throughout, cut out desired sections from transfer. **Note:** *Keep backs of pieces covered with protective paper until you are actually applying the transfer.* Arrange transfers on book cover, remembering that the right half of the cover will be the front, and the center will be on the book spine area.

2 Referring to manufacturer's instructions throughout, apply transfers one section at a time, starting with the spine. Remove protective paper, carefully position transfer slightly above surface of leather, and then lower into place. *Work carefully; parts of transfer may stick instantly, even before rubbing them.*

3 When all transfers are in place, paint the border of the book cover (between stitching and edge) with gold paint. Let dry.

4 Apply leather finish to completed project according to manufacturer's instructions to protect leather and transferred designs.

5 *Bookmark:* Turn under one end of ribbon 1 inch; glue or stitch loop to silk pansy and leaf. Turn under remaining end of ribbon 1 inch and glue inside book cover near spine. ◆

As a designer, I usually develop my own projects and designs from start to finish. However, sometimes it's fun to simply combine the wonderful products already designed by others that are widely available in craft stores.

—Sherian Frey

Antique Roses Dress Form

It's easy to add vintage charm to a dressing room or bedroom.
Add pretty pink roses to a dress form for an
instant decorating accent with Victorian flair!

Design by Lorine Mason

"I have always sewn and have long imagined a sewing room large enough to accommodate a wonderful collection of antique dress forms. This project might solve my space problem.
—**Lorine Mason**

Materials
- Papier-mâché dress form
- 14-inch (1/4-inch) dowel
- Small wooden finial to fit on end of dowel
- 3 x 5-inch oval wooden plaque
- Suede spray paint
- Metallic gold acrylic paint
- Spray of small (¾- to 1-inch) silk flowers with leaves to coordinate with decals
- Paintbrush
- Floral rub-on decals
- Varnish
- Craft drill with ¼-inch bit
- Painters tape or low-tack masking tape

Instructions

1. Mark center of wood plaque; drill hole at that point. Add a drop of glue and insert one end of dowel.

2. Drill or poke hole in center bottom and top of dress form. Thread dowel up through hole in bottom and out hole in top. Apply some glue to hole in finial; cap end of dowel. Apply more glue to bottom of finial; push dress form up into glue and secure until glue is dry.

3. Referring to photo throughout, pencil a curved line down length of dress form on front and back. Using tape, mask off left side of dress form, placing tape along curved line. Following manufacturer's instructions, spray right side of dress form, dowel and top surface of plaque with suede-finish paint. Let dry, then apply a second coat. Let dry; remove tape.

4. Paint left side of form, finial and remainder of plaque with gold paint. Let dry.

5. Cut apart decals to create clusters of flowers. Following manufacturer's instructions, rub decals randomly onto left (gold) side of dress form and onto the top of plaque.

6. Paint decals with varnish; let dry.

7. Separate leaves and flowers from spray. Glue along curved line on dress form. **Note:** If flowers seem too large, carefully trim away petals from back of flower. ◆

> **Create**
> Create a whimsical form by substituting dragonfly run-ons and using silk daisies in pinks and purples instead of the roses. A trendy form can be created in much the same way.

Flowers in a Row Pillow Box

Choose a rub-on transfer to fit the theme of the gift-giving occasion.

Design by June Fiechter

This is one of my favorite projects. I love the colors and the design. Even though it looks complicated, it is actually not difficult to create. Be sure to choose flowers that will fit on the size of box you choose. From there the sky is the limit!
—June Fiechter

Materials
- Cardboard pillow-style gift box
- 3 small silk flowers (sample uses individual petal layers separated from a larger flower)
- Rub-on transfer with desired wording
- Permanent adhesive
- Green thin suede lacing
- Acrylic craft paints: celery green, cream
- Awl
- 3 (⅛-inch) aluminum eyelets
- Sea sponge
- Hammer *and* metal paint scraper

Instructions

1 Referring to photo throughout, sponge celery green paint onto gift box, leaving some of the white background color showing through; let dry.

2 Sponge cream paint onto box, again leaving some of the white color showing; let dry.

3 Sponge on another coat of celery green; let dry.

4 Check fit of flowers across gift box; measure to space them evenly and lightly mark positions of flower centers on gift box. Using awl, poke small hole at each marked position.

5 Insert eyelet into center of each flower, then gently push a eyelet with flower into each hole. Hold metal scraper under eyelet (to protect back of box) and set eyelet by tapping it twice with hammer. Repeat to attach all flowers. Test flowers to make sure they are securely attached.

6 Cut transfer from sheet; trim around it closely. Following manufacturer's instructions, transfer it to box.

7 Insert gift in box; fold ends closed. Wrap suede lacing around box and tie ends in a bow on front. Trim ends. ◆

Create

Vary the look of the flowers by changing the style of eyelets you use to attach them. Choose from dozens of varieties that are available in scrapbooking stores.

Victorian Book Frame

Alter a book by cutting a photo frame into the cover.
Wrap it all up with a pretty ribbon.

Design by Mary Ayres

Materials
- Old book thick enough to stand on its end when closed—approximately 8 x 5¼ x 1¼ inches
- Pink floral rub-on transfer to fit on 2¼ x 3-inch rectangle
- 7 tiny white silk flowers removed from wire stems
- Leather chamois approximately the same size as front cover of book
- Approximately 1 yard 1½-inch-wide green wire-edge sheer ribbon
- Acrylic paints: white, light pink, dark pink, white pearl
- Paintbrushes
- White craft glue
- Photo to fit in 2¼ x 3-inch opening
- Fine sandpaper
- Metal-edge ruler
- Craft knife
- Cardboard

For this project, I wanted to make an altered book but wanted to keep the design details simpler than most of the designs I've seen. I decided to make a frame from the cover and not decorate the pages of the book at all. I thought the leather chamois had a very interested texture after scrunching it.

—Mary Ayres

Instructions

1 Using pencil, draw 2¼ x 3-inch vertical rectangle centered on top front of book cover. Place cardboard inside front cover. Cut drawn rectangle out of cover using craft knife and metal-edge ruler, and save rectangle to glue to bottom of cover later. Remove cardboard; smooth cut edges with sandpaper as needed.

2 Keeping book tightly closed, paint edges of pages white. Add a coat of white pearl; let dry.

3 Paint book cover and rectangle cut in step 1 with two or three smooth coats of light pink, allowing paint to dry between coats. Referring to instructions for dry-brushing (see "Painting Techniques," General Instructions, page 174), dry-brush edges of book, including cut opening and rectangle, with dark pink; let dry.

4 Paint chamois white on one side; let dry. Scrunch up painted chamois to give it texture, then lay flat.

5 From painted chamois, cut rectangle that is ½ inch smaller than front cover of book; cut 2¾ x 3½-inch rectangle from top of chamois so that cut-out opening in book cover will be in center of opening in chamois when chamois is centered atop book cover.

6 Dilute glue with a little water. Brush mixture onto back of painted chamois and press in place on front of book.

7 Rub flower transfer onto center of rectangle cut from book cover. Glue white silk flowers around transferred flowers. Glue rectangle across bottom of cover as shown; tape photo inside cover so it is visible through opening.

8 Wrap ribbon around center of book; tie ends in a bow under photo. Shape bow; trim ribbon ends evenly. ◆

Choose your favorite theme, whether Victorian, Oriental or funk. Choose the rub-on motif and florals to coordinate.

Create

Garden Sewing Trio

A coordinating needle book, pincushion and scissors fob are easy to create using scraps of faux suede. Floral rub-ons and a garland of tiny purple blossoms add a romantic touch to everyday accessories.

Design by Samantha McNesby

Materials
- Faux suede fabric: ¼ yard medium brown, scraps of burgundy
- Botanical rub-on transfers with lavender flowers
- Silk flowers: 1 yard wired green ivy, 1 stem small lavender flowers
- Craft paints: ivory, metallic gold, deep purple
- 1-inch wooden doll head
- 2 ½-inch wooden bowl
- 3-inch scallop-edge wooden medallion
- Foam brush
- Paintbrushes: ¼-inch flat, round detail brush
- Thick white craft glue *or* hot-glue gun
- Fiberfill
- Sewing supplies
- Iron

Painting & Transfers

1 Using foam brush, paint all wooden pieces with two coats ivory, letting paint dry between coats, Let dry.

2 Referring to photo throughout, apply botanical transfers to bowl, doll head and medallion, trimming transfers with scissors as needed.

3 Using ¼-inch paintbrush, add deep purple stripes around rim on bowl and medallion's side. Using

detail brush, add fine gold line around base of bowl rim and in carved details on face of medallion. Let dry.

Scissors Fob

1 Cut 8-inch piece wired ivy.

2 Fold ivory ribbon in half; knot ends together, creating a loop.

3 Trace 8-inch circle onto brown fabric; cut out.

4 Place circle right side down on flat work surface. Gather wad of fiberfill into tight ball about the size of a golf ball; place in center of fabric along with knotted end of ribbon loop. Gather fabric edges around ball and loop and wrap wired ivy tightly around gathers, twisting for a tight fit. Trim with scissors.

5 Clip lavender flowers from stem and glue them in place between ivy leaves; let dry.

6 Glue doll head to bottom of fob, with flat end against fabric; let dry.

Pincushion

1 Cut 12-inch piece wired ivy.

2 Trace 8-inch circle onto brown fabric; cut out.

3 Place circle right side down on flat work surface. Gather wad of fiberfill into tight ball about the size of a golf ball; place in center of fabric and gather fabric edges around it. Apply glue inside wooden bowl and place ball in bowl, gathered side down. Let dry.

Continued on page 173

French Country Floral Clock

All of the various elements in this design come together in a very striking accent piece. The grapes and crackle finish contribute to the elegant French country look.

Design by Vicki Schreiner

Materials

- Wooden carriage clock
- Clock movement with hands
- Acrylic paints: buttercream, grayish green
- Crackle medium
- Exterior/interior varnish
- 2 large pieces beige suede trim
- ⅛-inch suede leather laces: pink, sage
- Rub-on ivy transfers
- Assorted silk flowers and grape clusters
- ½-inch flat paintbrush
- Leather cement
- Fabric adhesive
- Low-temp glue gun
- Leather shears
- Wire cutters
- Craft knife
- Ballpoint pen
- Fine-grit sandpaper
- Tack cloth

> *Romance inspired this clock—and romance is timeless. You can easily achieve that vintage romantic look with the soft look of suede, the aged look of crackling and a few delicate flowers.*
>
> **—Vicki Schreiner**

Paint & Crackle Clock

1 Sand clock as needed; wipe off dust with tack cloth. Base-coat entire surface of clock except for face with two coats grayish green, letting paint dry between coats.

2 Referring to photo throughout, paint one coat of buttercream over grayish green on clock's square sides and outer edge.

3 Following manufacturer's instructions throughout, apply crackle medium to central frame of clock, working on one surface at a time—left side, right side and then front outermost edge. Let dry well.

4 Touch up any grayish-green areas as needed; let dry.

5 Apply one coat of varnish to entire clock except face; let dry.

Leather Pieces

1 Using ruler and ballpoint pen, measure pieces onto beige suede and cut out with shears: 2⅞ x 9⅛-inch piece for top of clock; 6½-inch square for clock face; two 8⅞ x ⁷⁄₁₆-inch strips; four 2¾ x ½-inch strips.

2 Miter ends of both 8⅞ x ⁷⁄₁₆-inch pieces as shown in Fig. 1; miter one end of two 2¾ x ½-inch pieces as shown in Fig. 2; miter one end of remaining 2¾ x ½-inch strips as shown in Fig. 3.

3 Referring to leather cement manufacturer's instructions, attach leather to clock, applying 2⅞ x 9⅛-inch piece to top of clock;

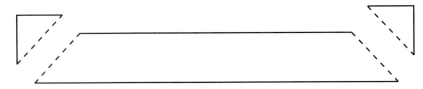

Fig. 1

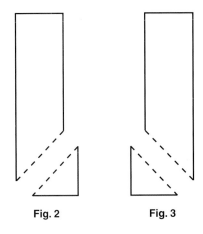

Fig. 2   **Fig. 3**

6½-inch square to clock face; and mitered strips to flat horizontal surfaces protruding at top and bottom of

clock, matching mitered corners neatly. Take care not to get any cement on right side of leather pieces; it will leave a mark.

Finishing

1 Following manufacturer's instructions, apply rub-on transfers to suede clock face as desired.

2 Following clock manufacturer's instructions, assemble clock movement and mount in clock.

3 Using leather cement and sage leather lace, make four ⅝-inch-

wide tight coils. Cement sage coils to clock face, measuring 1⅜ inches out from center and gluing coils at 12, 3, 6 and 9 o'clock positions.

4 Using craft knife, cut eight ⅜-inch pieces of pink leather lace. Cement pink pieces to 1, 2, 4, 5, 7, 8, 10 and 11 o'clock positions as shown.

5 Carefully cement one long piece of pink suede lace along each outer edge of clock face.

6 Using glue gun and wire cutters, attach flowers and grape clusters to top left corner and bottom right corner of clock as desired. As you work, reinforce hot glue with craft cement. ◆

Garden Sewing Trio
Continued from page 171

4 Wrap wired ivy tightly around top of bowl, twisting ends together for a tight fit. Trim off excess.

5 Clip lavender flowers from stem and glue them in place between ivy leaves; let dry.

Needle Book

1 Cut 12-inch piece wired ivy.

2 Cut two 9 x 5-inch rectangles from brown fabric and one 7 x 3-inch rectangle from burgundy.

3 Stitch brown rectangles together using ¼-inch seam allowance and keeping right sides together and edges aligned; leave a small opening

for turning. Turn right side out and press; hand-stitch opening closed. Fold piece in half; press.

4 Apply glue to back of wooden medallion; place on front cover of brown fabric "book," centering it carefully. Let dry.

5 Open needle book; place bur-gundy fabric inside. Add a strip of glue along center crease of open book; place burgundy

fabric right side up on top of glue. Let dry.

6 Wrap wired ivy around spine and inside the book; twist ends together for a tight fit, Trim off excess.

7 Clip lavender flowers from stem and glue them in place between ivy leaves; let dry.

8 Insert needles in burgundy fabric inside book. ◆

" I love making pretty sewing supplies—they make great gifts, and it is nice to make functional things to look at as well as use. I chose the transfers I liked, keeping in mind the smaller scale of my pieces, and selected a color scheme that worked around the transfers. My original idea was to use ivory faux suede, but once I arrived at the fabric store, the rich brown looked much better with the other colors I had chosen. "
—Samantha McNesby

General Instructions

Materials
In addition to the materials listed for each craft, some of the following supplies may be needed to complete your projects. Gather them before you begin working so that you'll be able to complete each design without a hitch!

General Crafts
- Scissors
- Pencil
- Ruler
- Paper
- Tracing paper
- Craft knife
- Paper towels
- Craft cutters *or* wire nippers
- Sheets of paper for catching and funneling glitter, microbreads, etc.
- Newspapers to protect work surface
- Safety pins, straight pins, tacks, etc.

Painted Items
- Large cardboard box or pieces of cardboard to contain overspray from spray painting
- Paper or foam plates for holding/mixing paints
- Plastic bags to protect work surface
- Recommended cleaner for brushes

Fabric Projects
- Iron and ironing board
- Press cloth
- Basic sewing notions and supplies
- Rotary cutter and self-healing mat
- Air-soluble markers
- Tailor's chalk

Save That Glitter!
Get the most from crafting supplies like glitter and tiny sequins. Work with one color at a time, and cover your work surface with a spare sheet of paper. After you've applied the glitter, tap off the excess onto the paper. Then, carefully fold the paper in half and funnel the excess glitter back into its container.

When working with microbeads, using a shallow lid (like a shoebox lid) for your work surface will keep the tiny beads from rolling away.

Spray Painting Made Simple
A large cardboard box (or a few large pieces of cardboard taped together) makes a nifty "booth" for spray-painting crafts. Make sure it's large enough to catch any overspray. It can be used again and again.

If you lay a dowel or stick across the top, you can suspend items in your booth for easier painting. You'll be able to spray all surfaces at the same time, cutting down on painting and drying time.

Small, lightweight items like wooden cutouts can be secured on loops of low-tack masking tape; stick them to the wall or floor of your painting area and spray. Let dry thoroughly.

Whenever you're using aerosol products (paint, varnish, sealer, etc.), work in a well-ventilated area—outside, if possible.

For a smooth, even, drip-free finish, apply spray paints in several light coats rather than one heavy one. Four to six light applications will yield a nicer finish—and you won't waste the paint that would drip off otherwise. Generally speaking, it's best to let paints dry between coats (unless otherwise instructed); most spray paints and other finishes dry quickly, especially when the ventilation is adequate.

Painted Designs
Disposable paper or plastic foam plates, including supermarket meat trays, make good palettes for pouring and mixing paints.

The success of a painted project often depends on the care taken in initial preparations, including sanding, applying primer and/or applying a base coat of color. Follow instructions carefully.

If you will be mixing media, such as drawing with marking pens on a painted surface, test the process and your materials on scraps to make sure there will be no running or bleeding.

Work in a well-ventilated area when using paints, solvents or finishes that emit fumes; read product labels thoroughly to be aware of any potential hazards and precautions.

Painting Techniques
Base coating: Load paintbrush evenly with color by dabbing it on palette, then coat surfaces with one or two smooth, solid coats of paint, letting paint dry between coats.

Dry brushing: Dip a dry round-bristle brush in paint; wipe excess paint off onto paper towel until brush is almost dry. Wipe brush across edges for subtle shading.

Stenciling with brush: Dip dry stencil brush in paint. Wipe brush on paper towel, removing excess paint to prevent seepage under stencil. Brush cutout areas with a circular motion, holding brush perpendicular to surface. When shading, brush should be almost dry, working only around edges. Use masking tape to hold stencil in place while working. ◆

Sources

Wood Bits, Stickers, Glitter, Glue, Spray Paint

All projects use Woodsies wooden cutouts from Forster.

Beads, Wires, Fibers, Paperclay & Powdered Pigments

All projects use Pearl-Ex powdered pigments from Jacquard Products.

Aztec-Influence Decorative Box

Rango Big Zoo rubber stamps from Red Castle Inc.

Candle Pedestal

Styrofoam brand plastic foam from Dow.

Floating Leaves Lamp Shade

Rubber Stampede aspen leaf stamp.

Kokopelli Candle

Kokopelli rubber stamp #E2065 from PSX Designs; Versamark stamping medium from Tsukineko Inc.

Looks-Great-With-Denim Necklace

Beadalon 49 flexible beading wire from Beadalon.

Wire-Adorned Mirror

Arnold Grummer's Paper Molds dragonfly #703 from Greg Markim Inc.

Plastic Foam, Mosaics, Paper, Feathers, Paint

All projects use Styrofoam brand plastic foam from Dow.

Fractured Sunflower Altered Book

Foam Finish from Beacon Adhesives.

Stamps, Clay, Metal, Embossing Powder, Glass Paint

Copper Accent Jewelry Set

ArtEmboss Metal copper sheet from AMACO; Crackled Background and Acanthus Background rubber stamps from Rubber Stampede; PermEnamel glass paints and clear gloss glaze from Delta; Embossing Pad and powders from Tsukineko.

Dressed-Up Terra-Cotta Pot

Ultrafrost Frosted Glass Paint from DecoArt; Lumiere Halo iridescent acrylic paint from Jacquard Products; Art Emboss Brass and WireMesh Copper from AMACO; Emboss Art embossing punch from McGill.

Ladybug Suncatcher

ArtEmboss red metal sheet from AMACO.

Oriental Wisdom Altered Book

"Long Life" stamp with border, "Fortune," "Friend" and "Joy" stamps all from Inkadinkado; "Long Life" rubber stamp from Stamp Francisco; Chinese coin, Chinese calligraphy and classic alphabet stamps all from All Night Media; Celtic alphabet stamps from PSX Designs; Archival Brilliance copper ink pad and Stayz-On ink pad for stamping on metal from Tsukineko; ArtEmboss copper sheet from AMACO; PermEnamel glass paint from Delta.

Summer Evening Candle Votive

ArtEmboss copper sheet and Metal Stamp Art ink pad, both from AMACO.

Verdigris Leaves Miniature Chimenea

Sculpey polymer clay and Translucent Liquid Sculpey from Polyform Products.

Plastic Foam, Mosaics, Paper, Feathers, Paint

Midnight Glitz Evening Bag

Bejeweler rhinestone setter from Creative Crystal Co.

Sparkly Summer Tote

Sequined butterfly Glamour Patch from BiGina.

Fabric & Window-Cling Paints

Autumn Leaves Frame

Paint Jewels window-cling paints and gold Liquid Lead from Delta.

Baby Scrapbook

Paint Jewels paints and gold liner Liquid Lead from Delta.

Coordinating Papier-Mâché Boxes

Liquid Laminate from Beacon; Paint Jewels window-cling paints from Delta.

Garden Window

Folk Art Crackle Medium, Gallery Glass Simulated Liquid Leading and Gallery Glass Window Colors, all from Plaid.

Gypsy Vase

Paint Jewels paints from Delta.

Shabby Chic Floral Pillow

Paint Jewels clear crystal paint and white Liquid Lead from Delta.

Spool Pincushion

Sudberry House spool pincushion; Paint Jewels paints from Delta.

Stained Glass Butterfly Box

Paint Jewels paints and Liquid Lead from Delta.

Stained Glass Toile Suncatcher

Liquid Rainbow Paints and Leading from DecoArt.

Sunshine & Posies Tissue Box

Liquid Rainbow paints from DecoArt.

Paper, Markers, Metallic Paints, Felt

Except as noted, all projects use Lumiere metallic paints from Jacquard Products.

Apple Canister

Green Apples #N10 napkin from DecoArt; Gallery Glass Crackle Medium #16047, Crystal Clear #16081 Window Color and Matte Medium #16048, all from Plaid.

Bath Salts in a Bottle

Stiffened Eazy Felt from CPE.

Embossed Roses Hanger Set

Kunin embossed felt.

Metallic Elegance Note Cards

Krylon 18K Gold Leafing pen.

Mod Circles Greeting Card & Envelope

Marvy Metallics markers from Marvy Uchida.

Polka-Dot Candle Lamps

Radiant Pearls pearlescent paint from Angelwings Enterprises.

Rub-On Transfers, Florals, Leather & Suede, Acrylic Paint

By the Sea Wastepaper Basket

Deerskin from Tandy Leather Co.; Fiskars rotary cutter with wave blade.

Floral Garden Book Cover

Tandy Leather book cover and Leather Sheen clear acrylic leather finish from The Leather Factory.

French Country Floral Clock

Carriage clock #5319 and Clock Movement with Hands #TQ600P from Walnut Hollow; suede trim, lace, Leathercraft cement and shears from The Leather Factory.

Buyer's Guide

Projects in this book were made using products provided by the manufacturers listed below. Look for the suggested products in your local craft- and art-supply stores. If unavailable, contact suppliers below. Some may be able to sell products directly to you; others may be able to refer you to retail sources.

Aitoh Co.
360 Swift Ave., No. 33
South San Francisco, CA 94080
(800) 681-5533
www.aitoh.com

All Night Media/ Plaid Enterprises
3225 Westech Dr.
Norcross, GA 80092-3500
(800) 842-4197
www.plaidonline.com

AMACO/American Art Clay Co. Inc.
4717 W. 16th St.
Indianapolis, IN 46222-2598
(800) 374-1600
www.amaco.com

Angelwings Enterprises
3322 W. Sussex Way
Fresno, CA 93722
(559) 229-1544
www.radiantpearls.com

Beacon Adhesives
125 MacQuesten Pkwy. S
Mount Vernon, NY 10550
(800) 865-7238
www.beacon1.com

Beadalon
(866) 4BEADALON
www.beadalon.com

ClearSnap Inc.
P.O. Box 98
Anacortes, WA 98221
(800) 448-4862
www.clearsnap.com

CPE
P.O. Box 649
541 Buffalo W. Springs Hwy.
Union, SC 29379
(864) 427-7900
www.cpe-felt.com

Creative Crystal Co.
6222 Tower Lane, Suite B-7
Sarasota, FL 34240
(800) 578-0716
www.bejeweler.com

D&CC
428 S. Zelta
Wichita, KS 67207
(800) 835-3013

DecoArt
P.O. Box 386
Stanford, KY 40484
(800) 367-3047
www.decoart.com

Delta Technical Coatings Inc.
2550 Pellissier Pl.
Whittier, CA 90601-1505
(800) 423-4135
www.deltacrafts.com

Design Master
P.O. Box 601
Boulder, CO 80306
(303) 443-5214
www.dmcolor.com

Diamond Tech International
5600-C Airport Blvd.
Tampa, FL 33634
(813) 806-2923
www.jennifersmosaics.com

Dover Publications
31 E. Second St.
Mineola, NY 11501-3852

Dow Chemical Co.
P.O. Box 1206
Midland, MI 48674
(800) 441-4369
www.dow.com

Duncan Enterprises
5673 E. Shields Ave.
Fresno, CA 93727
(800) 438-6226
www.duncancrafts.com

Elizabeth Ward & Co.
7855 Hayvenhurst Ave.
Van Nuys, CA 91406
(800) 727-2727

Fiskars Inc.
7811 W. Stewart Ave.
Wausau, WI 54401
(800) 950-0203, ext. 1277
www.fiskars.com

FloraCraft Corp.
P.O. Box 400
Ludington, MI 49431
www.floracraft.com

Forster Inc./ Diamond Brands
1800 Cloquet Ave.
Cloquet, MN 55720
(218) 879-6700
www.diamondbrands.com

Greg Markim Inc.
830 N. 109th St., Suite 22
Milwaukee, WI 53213
(800) 453-1485
www.arnoldgrummer.com

Highlander Celtic Stamps
(888) 999-2358
www.highlanderceltic stamps.com

Highsmith Inc.
W 5527 St. Rd. 106
P.O. Box 800
Fort Atkinson, WI 53538-0800
(800) 554-4661
www.highsmith.com

Inkadinkado
61 Holton St.
Woburn, MA 01801
(781) 938-6100
www.inkadinkado.com

Jacquard Products/Rupert, Gibbon & Spider Inc.
P.O. Box 425
Healdsburg, CA 95448
(800) 442-0455
www.jacquardproducts.com

Judi-Kins
17803 Harvard Blvd.
Gardena, CA 90248
(310) 515-1115
www.judikins.com

Krylon/Sherwin-Williams
W 101 Prospect Ave.
Cleveland, OH 44115
(800) 457-9566
www.krylon.com

Kunin Felt Co./ Foss Mfg. Co. Inc.
P.O. Box 5000
Hampton, NH 03843-5000
(603) 929-6100
www.kuninfelt.com

Leather Factory
P.O. Box 50429
Fort Worth, TX 76105
(817) 496-4414
(800) 433-3201
www.leatherfactory.com

Magic Scraps
1232 Exchange Dr.
Richardson, TX 75081
(972) 238-1830
www.magicscraps.com

Marvy Uchida of America Corp.
3535 Del Amo Blvd.
Torrance, CA 90503
(800) 541-5877
www.uchida.com

McGill Craftivity
Mail-order source:
Alpine Imports
7106 N. Alpine Rd.
Loves Park, IL 61111
(800) 654-6114

National Nonwovens
P.O. Box 150
Easthampton, MA 01027
(413) 527-3445
(800) 333-3469
www.nationalnonwovens.com

Plaid Enterprises Inc.
3225 Westech Dr.
Norcross, GA 30092-3500
(768) 291-8100
(800) 842-4197
www.plaidonline.com

Polyform Products Co./ Sculpey
1901 Estes Ave.
Elk Grove Village, IL 60007
www.sculpey.com

Provo Craft
Mail-order source:
Creative Express
295 W. Center St.
Provo, UT 85601-4436
(800) 563-8679
www.provocraft.com

PSX Designs
360 Sutton Pl.
Santa Rosa, CA 95407
(707) 588-8058
(800) 782-6748
www.psxdesigns.com

Ranger Industries Inc.
15 Park Rd.
Tinton Falls, NJ 07724
(800) 244-2211
www.rangerink.com

Red Castle Inc.
P.O. Box 1841
St. Cloud, MN 56302-1841
(877) RED-CASTLE
www.red-castle.com

Rubber Stampede Inc.
P.O. Box 246
Berkeley, CA 94701
(800) 423-4135
www.rstampede.com

Sakura Hobby Craft
2444 205th St., A-1
Torrance, CA 90501
(310) 212-7878
e-mail:
craftman@earthlink.net

Sanook Paper Co.
1367 Pacific Ave.
San Francisco, CA 94109
(415) 775-0971
www.sanookpaper.com

Stamp Francisco
308 S.E. 271st Ct.
Camas, WA 98607
(877) 268-4869
www.stampfrancisco.com

Syndicate Sales Inc.
2025 N. Wabash St.
P.O. Box 756
Kokomo, IN 46903-0756
(765) 457-7277
www.syndicatesales.com

Sudberry House
P.O. Box 895
East Lyme, CT 06371
(860) 739-6951

Tandy Leather Co.
100 Throckmorton St.,
Suite 1800
Fort Worth, TX 76119
(888) 890-1611
www.tandyleather.com

Therm O Web
770 Glenn Ave.
Wheeling, IL 60090
(847) 520-5200
www.thermoweb.com

Tsukineko
17640 N.E. 65th St.
Redmond, WA 98052
(800) 769-6633
(425) 883-7733
www.tsukineko.com

USArtQuest
7800 Ann Arbor Rd.
Grass Lake, MI 49240
(517) 522-6225

Walnut Hollow
1409 St. Rd. 23
Dodgeville, WI 53533-2112
(800) 950-5101
www.walnuthollow.com

Zucker Feather Products
P.O. Box 331
28419 Hwy. 87
California, MO 65018
(573) 796-2183

Designer Index

Mary Ayres
Dream Frame
Floral Memory Book
Gemstone Treasure Box
Stained Glass Toile Suncatcher
Victorian Book Frame
X's & O's Frame

June Fiechter
Antique Planter
Apple Canister
Bluebird Box
Elegant Gem Torchère
Flowers in a Row Pillow Box
Nature Mosaic Table
Nautical Adventures Frame
Seashore Bookend
Simple Flower Chest of Drawers
Southwest Accent Vase
Sunshine & Posies Tissue Box
Trailing Vines Portfolio
Words to Inspire Clock

Sherian Frey
Floral Garden Book Cover
Frosted Dragonflies Tray
Ladybug Suncatcher
Stained Glass Butterfly Box
Victorian Beaded Lamp Shade

Lisa Galvin
Bath Salts in a Bottle
By the Sea Wastepaper Basket
Contemporary Shadow Box
Fisherman's Theme Creel
Garden Window
Perky Daisy Tissue Box Cover
Summer Evening Candle Votive
Wire-Adorned Mirror

Katie Hacker
Buttons & Blocks Greeting Set
Geometric Key Holder
Glitter-Girl Photo Box
Harlequin Photo Tray
Looks-Great-With-Denim Necklace
Oriental Wisdom Altered Book
Travel Memories Photo Album

Judi Kauffman
Abstract Iris Vase
Asian Serenity Box
Aztec Influence Decorative Box
It's a Pot—It's a Table
Japanese Garden Chest of Drawers
Magnet Quartet
Manhattan Desk Set
Moonscape With Leaves Portfolio
My Eccentric Garden
Seaside Stories Bookend
Spool Pincushion
Time for Jewelry

Chris Malone
Botanical Garden Box
Collaged Garden Journal
Fun & Funky Purse
Fractured Sunflower Altered Book
Metallic Elegance Note Cards
Polka-Dot Treasure Box

Mary Lynn Maloney
Art Deco Brooches
Celtic Trinket Box
Color Wash Vase
Colors of Nature Collage
Dressed-Up Terra-Cotta Pot
Fabric & Fibers Planter
Family History Portfolio
Fringy Beaded Choker
Glamour Girl Lipstick Mirror
Gypsy Vase
Midnight Glitz Evening Bag
Mod Circles Greeting Card & Envelope
Playtime Pendulum Clock
Spring Blossoms Chest of Drawers
Suede Waves Bookend

Lorine Mason
Antique Roses Dress Form
Baby Scrapbook
Blazing Sun Garden Thermometer
Embossed Roses Hangers
Paper Roses Potpourri Ball
Romantic Rose Candle

Samantha McNesby
Dresden Set
Fantasy Fairy Doll
Garden Sewing Trio
Polka-Dot Candle Lamps
Princess Memory Box
Tag Trio
Trailing Vine Steppingstone

Sharon M. Reinhart
Cheery Cherry Wall Plaque
Gold-Studded Frame
Golden Pears Recipe Box
Kokopelli Candle
Sunflower Frame

Sandy L. Rollinger
Autumn Leaves Frame
Fantasy Dragonfly Candleholders
Out of Africa Lamp
Serene Reflections Set
Treasure Bottles
Verdigris Leaves Miniature Chimenea

Koren Russell
Candle Pedestal
Gilded Stucco Treasure Box
Guest Tote
Shabby Chic Floral Pillow

Vicki Schreiner
Coordinating Papier-Mâché Boxes
Copper Accent Jewelry Set
Floating Leaves Lamp Shade
French Country Floral Clock
Garden Creatures Button Covers
Sparkly Summer Tote